How Not
to Miss
the Point

How Not to Miss the Point

THE BUDDHA'S WISDOM
FOR A LIFE WELL LIVED

Jetsun Khandro Rinpoche

SHAMBHALA

Shambhala Publications, Inc.
2129 13th Street
Boulder, Colorado 80302
www.shambhala.com

Cover art: iStock.com/ProVectors
Cover design: Lauren Michelle Smith
Interior design: Kate Huber-Parker

9 8 7 6 5 4 3 2 1

First Edition
Printed in the United States of America

Shambhala Publications makes every effort
to print on acid-free, recycled paper.
Shambhala Publications is distributed worldwide by
Penguin Random House, Inc., and its subsidiaries.

Library of Congress Cataloging-in-Publication Data
Names: Rinpoche, Khandro (author)
Title: How not to miss the point: the Buddha's wisdom for a life well lived /
Khandro Rinpoche.
Description: First edition. | Boulder: Shambhala, 2025 |
Identifiers: LCCN 2024029463 | ISBN 9781611808568 (trade paperback)
Subjects: LCSH: Buddhism—Philosophy | Buddhism—Doctrines
Classification: LCC BQ4040 .R56 2025 | DDC 294.301—dc23/eng
LC record available at https://lccn.loc.gov/2024029463

The authorized representative in the EU for product safety and compliance
is eucomply OÜ, Pärnu mnt 139b-14, 11317 Tallinn, Estonia,
hello@eucompliancepartner.com.

Dedicated to Jetsunla, my sister, whose brilliant wisdom, vast vision, ability to bridge East and West, and unwavering dedication to the lineage and Dharma have been an extraordinary influence on all who have been fortunate to know you.

Contents

Editor's Preface

When the day came to try to describe this compelling book, it so happened that the Kentucky Derby, a pivotal US horse racing event, was taking place. Seen from the perspective of *How Not to Miss the Point*, this famously fast race was notable for one thing: the heartbreaking display of courage and determination of the fine animals themselves. It was heartbreaking because these qualities are so like our own. These are the qualities that "win the day." But they also beg the questions: What is the cup we are all racing for? How do we get to the goal we truly long to reach? And what does it mean to "live well" along the way?

How Not to Miss the Point is a straightforward message from Mindrolling Jetsun Khandro Rinpoche to anyone seriously looking for answers to these questions. These are the questions raised by the Buddha himself, with answers in the form of singular insight into the happiness that we human beings strive for and the way to actually realize it.

In part 1 of this book, Rinpoche encapsulates the traditional and elegantly simple arc of the Buddhist path of practice—and makes clear why this path is not necessarily Buddhist. It is, she explains, a path based on the most basic laws of nature: impermanence, interdependence, and the fact of "no-thingness," or lack of a solid self. When these verifiable truths are understood, the brilliant potential and basic goodness of human beings manifest. When they are ignored, the path itself identifies "in an almost allegorical way" the cause of suffering and the way to end it. Traditionally, these natural laws are referred to as Dharma: the truth of things as they really are. Their importance lies in their power to shape our lives and our world, individually and collectively, for the good.

Twenty-five hundred years ago, the Buddha came to realize these fundamental truths; and, moreover, he realized them to be universally true. With that realization came a shift in perspective: a turning of the mind from an outer to an inner source of truth and genuine contentment. Here, Rinpoche makes clear that "turning the mind inward" refers not to an escape but to a discovery uniquely made through working with one's own mind, observations, and experience. Why should the Buddha's discovery matter to us today? What impact could his teachings have on social norms or the shaping of kinder, more nurturing world cultures? And how and why would any personal or planetary happiness begin with a shift in my own perspective? In a clear and relatable manner, Rinpoche addresses the enduring questions that arise in the beginning, middle, and end of this endeavor.

Part 2 goes more deeply into what it means to put one's understanding of Dharma into practice. Given our lives in the world today, what key supports are needed by someone new to the path of practice? There are teachers, teachings, sanghas, and various styles of presenting the path. Rinpoche offers guidance for close consideration of those we encounter. In this way, an informed shift can be made from intellectual understanding to actually embodying the Buddha's wisdom.

For seasoned practitioners, one is reminded of the ongoing creativity of this transformative shift in perspective: the very heart of Buddhadharma. For the longtime practitioner who may have lost heart along the way, here that original inspiration may be rekindled. And for all readers, this book offers a realistic approach to bringing spirituality into our lives in a genuinely beneficial way.

How Not to Miss the Point draws on formal Buddhist teachings given in North America and Europe, as well as on informal conversations and stories, and is a story in and of itself. I say this because the committing of informal teachings to print is not truly compatible with the style of Jetsun Khandro Rinpoche or, for that matter, the Mindrolling lineage. While known for the profundity of its teachings and the exquisite ritual practices that embody them, the profile of Mindrolling lineage holders is traditionally flexible and low-key. In keeping with this tradition, Rinpoche has always been reluctant for such informal teachings to be "writ in stone." While wisdom itself is unchanging and timeless, the transmission of wisdom is always within the context of a particular time and place, addressed to a particular person or group of people. Therefore, such teachings always rely on the skillful means of receptivity and flexibility, qualities difficult to maintain when words get stuck in an unchanging context. With this understanding, we are extremely grateful to Rinpoche for her willingness for this small book to go forward and most especially for the timeless wisdom and skillful relevance ever present in her teachings.

Before there were any books, the sharing of this wisdom was an oral tradition passed on from teacher to student. Historically, great teachers and teachings challenged students to question and to verify the truth of these simple teachings for themselves. Thus, based on our varying inclinations and potentials, the understanding and expression of essential wisdom has become abundantly diverse. This is the good news.

The main challenge then as now—and as reflected in these pages—is the need to get to the heart of the matter. Through the kindness and generosity of Jetsun Khandro Rinpoche, the simple why and how to do so is offered in a way that speaks to all readers, Buddhist and non-Buddhist, new and old practitioners. For me personally, these teachings have greatly deepened my own understanding and remain a source of great gratitude to Rinpoche, who so kindly bestowed them. For any errors in the sharing of these teachings, I take full responsibility. May their indestructible wisdom be of immeasurable benefit.

Helen Berliner
Mindrolling Lotus Garden
Stanley, Virginia
2024

Preface

The challenge today is to take the immense interest in spirituality out of the realm of intellectual appreciation and into our lives in a way that is realistically beneficial.

It seems that almost every day of my life is spent with people throughout the world who all show great interest in studying and practicing the Buddha's teachings. Some are dedicated, formal Buddhist practitioners, but many are not. The more you learn about the Buddha's teachings, the more you should come to understand that being a Buddhist doesn't rely on practices, forms, and other formalities; it relies on realizing the meaning and intent of these teachings.

But what was the Buddha's intent? And what does that have to do with our own lives and the difficult world we are living in today? Given the speed of radical change occurring globally, socially, and economically, who doesn't feel a sense of chaos and imbalance? The challenge today is to take the immense interest in spirituality out of the realm of intellectual appreciation and into our lives in a way that is realistically beneficial.

This is the challenge that first motivated the Buddha. The Buddha's intent was never to create Buddhism. The intent had to do with uncovering the intrinsic goodness, kindness, and happiness within us—and whatever is standing in the way of that.

THE INTRINSIC GROUND OF GOODNESS

The Buddha's enlightenment had nothing to do with becoming something or someone else. It had to do with recognizing the intrinsic human nature, which is absolute truth. Call it basic goodness, intrinsic wisdom, or buddha nature—from the ultimate point of view and from the very beginning—this is the innate nature of all sentient beings. And this is the core essence of Buddhist understanding and practice. But what can one say about absolute truth?

When I was growing up, I was very lucky to attend a Catholic convent school for half of each day and to experience that form of education. The Catholic nuns were generous, kind, and very simple and direct: "You should do this and not do that; and do it this way, not that way." For me, this was very nice because the other half day was spent studying Dharma in the monastery, where nothing that one said seemed to be right. This was especially true during my rebellious teen years, when we were learning the logic of Madhyamaka.

Madhyamaka is the basic Buddhist logic of philosophical examination. It deals primarily with absolute truth and the impossibility of expressing absolute truth in a concept. As in some Greek philosophies, the truth can never be stated; whatever is stated to be truth is simply refuted. Thus one cannot say what truth is; one can only say what truth is not.

For a teenager, never getting a pat answer was very frustrating: "This isn't right, that's not right; it's a fabrication, a mental concept, a thought. Yes, its nature is emptiness, but no, it is not empty. And what is a thought?" No matter what answer you come up with, it is not right, and holding on to it could be seen as grasping or arrogance. The frustration grew, and I finally went to His Holiness Mindrolling Trichen, my root teacher and father, and asked, "Why is Buddhism so complicated? It seems so unnecessarily complicated."

To this Rinpoche replied, "When the Buddha attained realization and enlightenment, he tried to expound on what he found to be true, but no one seemed to understand." It is said that for almost seven weeks thereafter, the Buddha did not teach. Finally, he began teaching what is now known as the origin of Buddhism, or the first turning of the wheel of Dharma. Then there was the second turning of the Wheel, and the Buddha's many later teachings are referred to as the third turning of the wheel of Dharma.

Today, the simplicity of what the Buddha taught in the first and second turnings may seem almost ironic. We are told there is suffering. There is a cause of suffering. And should we want suffering to cease, there is a path of practice that leads us from the cause to the cessation of suffering. It is very simple. Yet, thus began a very complex philosophy.

Growing up, I always blamed that first group of people who failed to understand what the Buddha actually discovered. Had they just been able to comprehend a direct presentation of absolute truth, we would not now have to suffer all the analysis, meditation, methods, rituals, and highly complex philosophy that is Buddhism today! But in all seriousness, the truth of suffering and its cause are as true today as they were two thousand five hundred years ago. And in order to fully realize the goodness, kindness, and happiness within us, we need to understand them.

Having realized the cause of suffering and its cessation to be universally true, the Buddha saw the fundamental responsibility of a human being. If we would like our own lives, the lives of others, and the life of our planet to be fulfilling and good, we must accept responsibility for cultivating the best qualities of our human minds and conduct. As you read on, you will see how and why this is so.

The intent of the Buddha's teachings was to convey the truth of this responsibility. To put this perspective into practice, the need to tame the mind and the importance of meditation were taught. You don't have to be a Buddhist to understand this perspective and practice. By relying on direct experience and your own wisdom mind, you are basically doing what the Buddha himself did.

What the Buddha taught about the potential of the human mind and its qualities is not necessarily Buddhist. Any teaching or method, Buddhist or not, that helps us develop such qualities deserves great appreciation. Any teaching that helps us locate our intrinsic goodness and contentment instead of relentlessly pursuing happiness externally is absolutely wonderful. The increasing interest in meditation and contemplation is wonderful. For the world's population to persevere in displaying its good human qualities and to coexist with some amount of sanity is wonderful.

Because some of these teachings just happen to be the teachings of Shakyamuni Buddha, many of us who practice them refer to ourselves as Buddhist practitioners. At some point, the reference to being Buddhist becomes irrelevant, but for now we have that label.

BRINGING MEANINGFUL
THEORIES DOWN TO EARTH

For many years, my Western Buddhist friends have tried to convince me that it is possible to balance this challenging world and the spiritual path: what we call "samsara and nirvana." They use the image of an untainted lotus growing pristine and pure from muddy waters. I joke with them about this because my take on this beautiful image is that in today's times, the lotus tends to be splattered with mud, and our lofty philosophies, both sacred and secular, tend to be naive.

How then can we bring these very meaningful theories down to earth in a way that results in true and proper change for the good with benefits that are directly accessible to ourselves and others?

This was the challenge faced by the Buddha himself. Raised as the son of a king, the Buddha began to question the lack of genuine satisfaction found in palace life, in society, and on the spiritual paths presented to him. His dissatisfaction was not so much with religion or philosophy but rather with the way that human beings related to them. It all came down to seeing the solution to unhappiness and suffering to be extrinsic—which the Buddha questioned. His questioning led to a shift in perspective toward finding answers within.

This insight took into account the "mud" of a human being's lifetimes of neurotic patterns, as well as our inherent nature of goodness. It took into account the challenges of our worldly and spiritual, individual and interconnected lives. It therefore took into account the responsibility we have as human beings to abandon the cause of suffering and to cultivate what is intrinsically good. This was the Buddha's definition of "social responsibility." Conveying the truth of this responsibility was the Buddha's intent for the benefit of all beings—non-Buddhists and Buddhists alike. These are the teachings that came to be known as Buddhadharma and, in practice, Buddhism.

This small book focuses on the simplicity of the Buddha's insight and advice. For those of you newly interested in the Buddhist path, it could serve as a simple map and guide. For longtime practitioners, it offers a reminder of the simplicity of the Buddha's transformative shift in perspective. And for those who may have run out of steam along the way, it might remind you of your original inspiration. For all readers, it offers a realistic approach to bringing spirituality into our lives in a genuinely beneficial way.

And so, as we human beings are wont to do, we will say more about the simplicity of the Buddha's teachings.

PART ONE

The Buddha's Advice
for a Meaningful Life

ONE

What Is the Essence of Buddhism?

IF YOU HAPPEN TO BE a Buddhist practitioner, nothing more may need to be said about the essence of Buddhism. But when I ask myself what the essence of Buddhism is, I find that certain things do need to be said about what the Buddha taught and what we practice. For those of us who have been practicing Dharma for many years, it may be even more important to sit back and ask ourselves what the essence of Buddhism truly is. If we don't, we may suppose we know what we're doing, meanwhile missing the point. Let me explain.

I was in a food court recently with a group of monks and nuns, seated at various tables. As we were eating, two young fundamentalist Christians walked up to one of the tables and began asking the monks and nuns about Buddhism and suggesting they repent. I busied myself with my noodles but kept an ear out for how their questions would be answered. The answers were all good ones. Many of us would have answered the same way: Buddhism is about recognizing your own basically good nature and wisdom. It is about compassion and all the other words we have heard before. But this set me to thinking, "What does Dharma really mean to us? And what do Buddhists really do?"

I get these questions almost every week of my life from the immigration officers at the airport: "What do you do? What is your profession?" I usually say, "I'm a Buddhist nun." And the officer stamping passports usually responds, "Oh, okay," which makes me wonder what exactly he thinks I do. What is a nun's job? Beyond some vague sense of what a nun is, is there any depth of understanding? Likewise, the answers we rattle off when asked about Buddhism often give some vague impression or are simply textually correct. But how often are they just distancing us from what Buddhism actually is?

CHECKING THE CORRECT ANSWERS
OR NONE OF THE ABOVE

These days there are many conceptual ideas about what it means to be a Buddhist. We may call ourselves Zen Buddhists or Tibetan Buddhists, Vajrayana, or Mahayana practitioners. We say that Buddhism is about compassion. The very thought of compassion has substance, and so we may believe that label is sufficient. Psychologically, our minds are very susceptible to labels and concepts.

What does a Buddhist do? If we were asked the question on an exam, we would check the correct answers. "We chant and meditate." What do we meditate on? "The nature of mind." What is the nature of mind? "It's empty." Such answers, however, are not particularly heartfelt. They are not about something that we really know the taste of. So even if you do practice and have some understanding of the teachings, you may need to sit down with your conceptual ideas and look at what it truly means to be a Buddhist.

If we go back to the beginning, Buddhism was not Buddhism, and the Buddha never turned anyone into a Buddhist because the word didn't exist. In the beginning, Buddhism was not a philosophy, a science, or a religion. So what does it mean to call yourself a Buddhist? To be a Buddhist is to be absolutely honest and true to the best that a human mind has to offer. If you can do that without a moment of formal meditation or anything Dharmic—absolutely do it! That is how it should be. But given lifetimes of habitual neurotic patterns and all of today's difficulties and outer distractions, the support of a step-by-step approach might make more sense. In this case, you could follow in the footsteps of great beings over the last two thousand five hundred years—and you could do it well.

If you walk into any bookstore today or just browse the internet, you will find countless ways to make your life better. There is some purpose and goodness to this. You can find ways to cure your ills, to understand one another better, or to simply make your weekends more relaxing. Buddhism too has become better known and more accessible. Beyond the traditional philosophy and advanced teachings, many are now familiar with the teachings on compassion, the practice of meditation, and the Buddhist view.

The downside to this rapidly growing interest is that it may not be properly guided or in depth. When we talk about any philosophy and way of life, we are talking about something very precious. This is something we should consider seriously and carefully and not as just a fashionable curiosity. Understanding the value of whatever we are about to adopt into our minds and lives requires careful thought and reflection. Attraction to the outer form of any philosophy or way of life poses the danger of not understanding its true meaning and intent. And with something as profound as the study and practice of Buddhism, this lack of understanding will prevent us from deriving any real benefit.

In order to understand the indisputable truth and benefit of Dharma, I encourage you to take the support of the two thousand five hundred years of wisdom teachings, the depth and richness of the classical texts, and the example of those great ones who brought this understanding to fruition for the benefit of all beings.

CANDYFLOSS AND TREADMILL BUDDHISTS

While traveling in Europe a while ago, I happened to watch a television interview with a French politician who was airing her views on religious attire. The wearing of a hijab in public was a big part of the conversation, as was the wearing of yarmulkes by Jewish men. Of course, what would one then do with the Catholic nuns and monks? As a Buddhist nun, I began to think that by next year I might have to wear a wig.

That conversation spoke to bigger questions: What is religion? What does it mean to call yourself a Buddhist, and what does a Buddhist actually do? Sometimes these questions are sincere, but often there's a certain tone to the question, the same tone one might use to ask a friend, "Why ever would you dye your hair pink?" In this case, you must have a good answer, not only for their sake but for your own sake as well. Your answer must be truly honest and experiential because that kind of answer will become the basis of your confidence on the path.

Today there is much talk of the growing culture of Buddhism-lite. This is a kind of Buddhist fluff, like lace doilies or sweet pink blossoms in the spring. I call it the "candyfloss" (or cotton candy) kind of Buddhism. It's very eye-catching and cute. There is much fondness for the various cultural trappings and outer accoutrements of formal practice. Often there is also a goal-oriented approach to mindfulness meditation. The people are quite sweet, and it does serve some purpose. But in terms of our actual potential, relying on the outer aspects of any spiritual path is quite limiting.

Beyond an emotional connection, flowery feel-good Buddhism lacks the depth and direct experience of the meaning of the Buddha's teachings. It may lead to a certain gentle understanding, especially in the beginning. Like caffeine or chocolate, it may be good for weekend programs, for writing good articles, or for bringing people in. But it is not powerful enough to eradicate lifetimes of neurosis. And in this age of rapid dissemination of information, it can miss the point, which, in the case of Buddhism, is profound and transformative.

For this reason, one might be very sharp with people who promote fluff and those who profit from it. But instinctively one wants to say, "It's all right." There may be some benefit. It may plant a seed, and some of these candyfloss Buddhists are our good friends.

There is another group, who I call the treadmill Buddhists. This kind of Buddhist is very diligent, learned, and capable. They are also very busy being focused, spiritual, and really holy: "Now, I am really going to do it. I'm going for it now!"

And then there are the rest of us. If we don't fit into either of these groups, what are we doing? We too may be studying and practicing, trying to gain wisdom, be kind, and observe the nature of mind. But what does a living, breathing Buddhist do beyond all this? From a Buddhist perspective, it doesn't much matter whether you wear a scarf, a yarmulke, or have hair on your head. Such differences aren't important. So, what is the difference between you and the person sitting next to you on the bus?

The difference is your perspective, or view. If you call yourself a Buddhist, it is your responsibility to examine this: What is your view on life? What is your view of yourself, your relationships, your journey—and how is this view any different from that of someone who may never have met with the Dharma? Moreover, does your Buddhist perspective have the flavor of direct experience? Or, are you merely looking through someone else's tinted glasses?

FAITHFUL FOLLOWERS

A view left unchallenged becomes dogmatic and systematic. Compassion, for example, is something that all Buddhists—candyfloss Buddhists, treadmill Buddhists, and the rest of us—talk about. It is almost synonymous with being a Buddhist. But what is your perspective on compassion? You could surely give a sensible answer if asked. Try talking about compassion with other Buddhists. We've heard it, we like it, we believe in it, we repeat it. And this makes us true believers. Suppressed by dogma, you could become a faithful follower of a profound belief, without the discriminating mind or freedom to ever have a direct experience and without the courage to remain true to your own wisdom.

To not become this kind of follower, it is essential to shape your own discerning wisdom by examining, challenging, seeing clearly, and not viewing the truth as someone else's experience.

CONTEMPLATION

Working with your own mind and perspective on life is the very heartbeat of Dharma. You don't become a Buddhist to imitate outer forms or beliefs. You become a Buddhist to follow in the footsteps of the Buddha, and thus unearth the best of your own mind and life.

We Buddhists have become careless about this. Now we really need to keep it in mind. Otherwise we will wind up doing many things but not the most important thing: taming the mind to unearth its full potential. Please never lose sight of that.

THE BUDDHA'S SHIFT IN PERSPECTIVE

What the Buddha sought and found during his lifetime was a slightly different perspective on things. Instead of relying on extrinsic causes of happiness and suffering, he found that the true source of happiness and the cause of suffering were within oneself. From this perspective, he saw that one would cultivate a different kind of attitude and conduct.

This was a view that you could remain true to, no matter what worldly activities you engaged in or what background you came from. You could sustain your Brahman belief, Hindu belief, or whatever belief, if it worked with how you saw things. In his teachings today, His Holiness the Dalai Lama often refers to being a good Christian Buddhist, or a Muslim Buddhist, or a Hindu Buddhist. This isn't some clever tactic to convert people to Buddhism. It is absolutely true that you could be a good Christian Buddhist. A Buddhist is supposed to drop the term Buddhist. To become a non-Buddhist is the ultimate goal. What this means is that for someone who is truly Buddhist, the truth of impermanence, interdependence, and change is universal and beyond labels, even the label of "Buddhist." Ideally, this would be how the Buddha's heart teachings and intent would be lived and shared.

For Tibetans, the question of the Buddha being a Buddhist never comes up, as the word doesn't exist in the Tibetan language. It is an English word, so this is a fight that belongs more to the English-speaking West. In Tibetan, the term that is used for "Buddhist" is *nangpa sanggyepa* or simply *nangpa*. The term for a non-Buddhist would be *chirolpa* or *chipa*. Colloquially, *nangpa* means "insider," and *chipa* means "outsider." But more literally these terms could be translated as "intrinsic" and "extrinsic." A Buddhist would be someone who is open to working inwardly. On the other hand, one who searches for answers outwardly and puts all responsibility and blame outside of oneself would be called a non-Buddhist. So, if the Buddha worked with his intrinsic mind, he was a Buddhist.

A non-Buddhist might temporarily become a Buddhist in order to learn something from it and then become a non-Buddhist again. This "non-Buddhist," however, would be a very different person after seeing the reality of the nature of self and phenomena. This is the absolutely necessary shift in perspective that must be made. Ultimately, this non-Buddhist might come to be called a buddha, an awakened or enlightened one. This is how the Buddha himself evolved two thousand five hundred years ago.

Beyond the Influence of Systems and Cultures

The general accounts of the Buddha's life tell us that he grew up as a prince. As a young man, he was surprised to learn of birth, old age, sickness, and death, and so he went off to seek freedom from the suffering of birth, old age, sickness, and death. This is the general story. But let's take time to look at how the Buddha actually grew up.

At that time in India, there were many princely states called kingdoms and a culture of constantly warring clans. The kingdom into which the Buddha was born was not very big. Nevertheless, his father, King Shuddhodana, like all the kings, was driven to win over other kingdoms and become an emperor of sorts. On top of that, Prince Siddhartha was born very late to his parents. Today we would say they were young, but in olden times a king was supposed to have secured his kingdom with an heir by the age of eighteen.

By the time the ambitious King Shuddhodana finally had a son to be proud of, certain relatives missed their chance at the throne. So the young prince grew up surrounded not only by the luxuries of a princely life but also by his father's ambitions and the extreme jealousy, pride, strife, and hard feelings of his relatives. His own cousins would have gladly seen him dead. The starkness of all things good and all things bad—this was his upbringing.

Now the prince was very intelligent, and he had access to some of the most wonderful teachers of his time. It was this curious mind that became discontent and questioning. Beyond the suffering of birth, old age, sickness, and death, here he was living in the palace, day in and day out, with extreme ambition on the one hand and extreme jealousy on the other. This curious mind was led to seek answers to what it is we human beings are trying to do, and it was not satisfied with the great masters' answers. "It is destiny," they said. "This is how it is. You go along with the system or you abandon everything." It is significant that from this time on, the Buddha never sat on a throne nor claimed to be special. This is an essential characteristic of the Buddha and of Buddhism, itself. The thrones and shrines all came later.

Inevitably, whenever Buddhism goes to another country, there are cultural influences. There were cultural influences on Indian Buddhism, Chinese Buddhism, Japanese Buddhism, and the Buddhism of Vietnam and Sri Lanka. Today in the West, you may sit on a chair to hear the teachings. This probably didn't happen in the time of the Buddha. Buddhism moves with the times. Its content and context are uniquely expressed. As long as the core principles are kept, such changes are allowed to occur. This is one of the beauties of Buddhism.

Tibetan Buddhism is a very rich tradition. Historically, it was privileged to have had whole lineages of excellent scholars and masters from India and later from Tibet, who traveled back and forth to establish the teachings in Tibet. Beautifully blended into Tibetan Buddhism were many aspects of Tibet's own pre-Buddhist religions, as well as many qualities of the Hindu, Zen, and Chinese traditions. Also included were all three streams of the Buddha's teachings, known as the three *yanas*, or "vehicles": Hinayana, Mahayana, and Vajrayana.

In brief, these are three stages of understanding and practice. The Hinayana has to do with the taming of the unruly mind. The Mahayana emphasizes the recognition of the actually empty, or egoless, nature of self and others—which, when not recognized, is the cause of suffering. The Vajrayana focuses on one's inherently awake and basically good nature when freed from the delusion of a solid self: the wisdom essence of all Dharma teachings.

With all of its own struggles and challenges, Tibetan Buddhism is a blend of everything good that Buddhism has to offer. This may be why it does so well in the culturally diverse West. Like a beautiful garden, it offers many wonderful aspects and qualities of Buddhism. But is this the Buddhism that was there in the time of the Buddha? Yes and no. Yes, in that it tries to sustain the purity of the Buddha's lineage. Yes, in that it teaches nothing other than what the Buddha taught. No, because there are many cultural influences.

Unfortunately, these outer aspects are often emphasized more than the pure essence of Buddhism, as it was in the time of the Buddha. Becoming a monk or nun can become more important than Dharma. Sitting on a red cushion, or knowing how to strike a gong, or how to breathe can become more important than Dharma. We begin to think of ourselves as Mahayanists or Vajrayanists. And in the Vajrayana, it's endless: knowing when to ring a bell or how to visualize deities may be seen as Buddhism rather than the essence of Buddhism itself.

We then learn to shop for thrones and artwork and paints in all the right colors. This is all very nice to learn, but is it Buddhism? Definitely not. When this is what we emphasize, we forget what the Buddha taught—and why.

In the Face of Great
Goodness and Negativity

Two thousand five hundred years ago, there was actually no need for Buddhism to originate in India. India had a rich spiritual culture, with the most sophisticated thinking and philosophy, and everyone seemingly following a path of practice. There would have had to be a major reason for anyone to think, "I need to come up with something different." Yet, this is exactly what the Buddha thought. What is crucial to keep in mind is why the Buddha became dissatisfied with an already sophisticated form of spirituality.

Not only did the Buddha experience both great goodness and extreme negativity in his own life, he also experienced this in society. At that time, despite being such an evolved civilization spiritually and culturally, Indian society had begun to face its share of flaws. One was clan division. There were many clans who were all constantly trying to destroy each other and gain supremacy. The division among clans was immense.

The second was gender division. The society was becoming more and more patriarchal, and the situations faced by women were becoming extremely negative.

The third very negative defect was class division. The division between the upper classes—the Brahmans, the spiritually inclined, and the warriors—and the lower class of untouchables was extreme.

These three divisions struck the Buddha as being profoundly contradictory to any sophisticated spiritual belief. The Hindu tradition, for example, believed primarily in a pure self: the Brahman self, or ultimate consciousness, created by god. We are all of that pure self and should remain in the pure self. Externally, however, there were the divisions of clans, genders, and classes. These contradictions were extremely difficult for Siddhartha. They led to his asking questions and to his dissatisfaction with answers that were philosophically correct but contradictory in practice.

This made Siddhartha go beyond his own kingdom and his responsibilities as the heir, to follow the path of asceticism. For over six years, he studied and meditated with two main teachers, Arada Kalama and Udraka Ramaputra, before moving on to become the one known as the Buddha, the "awakened one."

AN AWAKENING

The Buddha's actual awakening was probably very simple: just a question, an answer, and a change of perspective.

To understand what the Buddha found to be true—which later became known as Buddhism—you have to ponder what it means to awaken. The origin of the word *buddha* is *budh* or *buddhi*, which simply means "awakened," or "to know better."

According to the Buddhist teachings, all sentient beings have minds but only a human being is endowed with the extraordinarily rare capacity to awaken to one's own mind. When an ordinary human being is able to go beyond thoughts and behaviors that are conditioned by ignorance, confusion, and lack of insight—that is an awakening. That human being is a buddha, an awakened one.

This is how the Buddha defined his own realization. It was not the eureka moment shown in TV documentaries and movies, with its thunder and lightning and demon attacks followed by sudden peace and flower petals showering down. The Buddha's actual awakening was probably very simple: just a question, an answer, and a change of perspective. That is an awakening. The enlightenment sound-and-light show—with its displays of clairvoyance, omniscience, and magic—is cinema. Buddhahood begins to seem very exotic, and we begin to think this is what we have to become. This drama has distanced buddhahood from who we are today.

I recently had the opportunity to have a very accomplished Tibetan physician check out some of our sangha members. Over the course of two or three days, he read the pulses of about a hundred Vajrayana practitioners. And what did he find? Most of them had one sickness in common: fear. They were all very afraid. There are some, of course, with real diseases such as cancer—and other real problems such as sleeplessness, anxiety, fibromyalgia, and so on. But the sickness common to all of them was fear.

We meditators are very scared people: scared of making mistakes, scared of grasping, scared of not being good enough, scared that meditation won't happen. We think we have to get to that buddhahood state and become a painting on the wall. Yet, here we are with our thoughts and distractions and no topknot.

All these imaginings make buddhahood and meditation seem very distant and difficult. We've seen the dramatic movies, but when we meditate, there is no thunder, no ringing of bells, and no goddesses showering flower petals. This creates a sense of great difficulty. We begin to imagine that the Buddha's six-year quest was extremely difficult, and we like to dramatize that. Six years, however, is not a long time. Many of you have been Buddhists much longer than that. So what is it that the Buddha found that we ourselves are not finding?

Finding What Is Applicable to Us Now

Today, it is popular to call meditation a "contemplative science" and to think that science must somehow prove Buddhist ideas. There are some similarities, of course, and the dialogue is helpful. But when it comes down to what really matters, Buddhism is not science. Certainly scientists would never say that it is. Why? Because the Buddha's teachings and the whole approach of Dharma are based on nonconceptual realization; there is no concrete evidence, which is the basis of any scientific belief. Therefore, Buddhism itself is not science. Moreover, Buddhism never claimed to be a religion, although religious people may not agree. And it is not entirely a system of psychology. Buddhism is not any of those things.

To find what is applicable to us now, we must go back to the original simplicity of the Buddha's perspective. To better understand this, it is important to keep two things in mind: the Buddha never claimed to be anything special, and he never claimed to be an intermediary to some higher being or higher self.

These days, more and more teachers are seen to be in some way special. The *tulku* system, for example, the tradition of recognizing incarnated masters, can be viewed in various ways. Yes, this system has its own uses, but when the system overrides the Dharma, we have a problem. Likewise, the notion of a spiritual intermediary—a clairvoyant, an omniscient one, a spiritual VIP—is a problem. These are the very problems originally encountered by the Buddha.

With more and more people practicing Dharma, it is important to be a bit skeptical about such things. Whatever doesn't sound like something the Buddha did during his lifetime probably should not be emphasized now. At a certain time and in a certain culture, certain things may have made sense. But times change. Remember too how the Dharma was taught. For the most part, Dharma was not taught in a lecture format with one person talking and all others listening. Occasionally, this format is very fine, but it was not the way the Buddhist teachings were traditionally imparted. The Buddha mainly engaged with his students through questions and answers, an approach that reflected the path itself.

On the path of Dharma, it is oneself—the subject, not the object—who must develop by engaging in the process. This cannot happen in a lecture format or through books. There you can pick up pointers, clues, and ideas, some of which may be very beneficial. But there is a gap between you and the teachings, like a wide-open back door that allows you to escape when you're challenged by habitual patterns, with all their reasonings and rhetoric. As a result, you may know a lot, but your knowledge is not what you live by. This is particularly unfortunate, since Buddhism was never intended to be a philosophy or belief.

The Simple and the Complex

From the very beginning, Buddhism was a nontheistic path with a very simple premise. It could be summed up as selfless compassion at all times. The term *selflessness* here means the dissolution of any tendency of the grasping mind to revert to habitual self-cherishing, which is the cause of suffering. This itself is true compassion. It is very simple, very logical. This is what the Buddha found to be true.

Selfless compassion—call it enlightenment or the realization of absolute truth—is the state beyond self-attachment and self-grasping. In practice, it is genuine kindness. To practice kindness, there is no need to adhere to any form. In fact, in the time of the Buddha, there was a strong emphasis on not bringing form into practice. However, to simply say, "Do this and it will lead to realization," presents enormous difficulties.

Going beyond self-attachment is not an easy or familiar thing to do. And because we human beings are enormously capable of complicating things, questions will always arise. By the time this simple teaching went from India to Tibet, the value of selfless compassion was understood. But then, if this is the goal of the path, how do we realize it? What is kindness? How is it actually practiced? And in the face of difficulties, doubt, or a mind that doesn't understand how to be selfless—what then? This left the Buddha no choice but to teach a simple subject in various complex ways.

It is humbling to think that we struggle today in the same ways that people struggled two thousand five hundred years ago. The human mind is curious and in need of structure and support. One could say this is why the enlightened buddhas and bodhisattvas manifest and teach. Their selfless motivation is the benefit of others. So when you ask a question, you will get an answer. In this way, the Buddha's formless, nontheistic philosophy found itself in need of a formatted path, a path with principles and practices to cultivate, activities to abandon, and so on. The various paths we have today are simply in response to the human mind that needs structure and support in order to understand the truth.

YOUR FREEDOM TO CHOOSE

This is the preciousness of a human life.

Basically, there is no difference between an ordinary human being and an awakened one. It wouldn't take you thirty seconds to go from ordinary to awake if you chose to do so. At every moment, you have the innate ability to choose how you look at things and to exercise that choice. You can choose to be conditioned by habitual assumptions, confusion, and misunderstanding, or you can free yourself from these conditions and see things as they are. The freedom to choose is what makes the human life such an exceptional gift.

This is the preciousness of a human life. To say that ordinary human beings are not fully awakened simply means that our true potential is covered over by conditioned thoughts and behaviors.

When I teach, for example, I am usually provided with a glass of water. The glass could just as easily be a paper cup, but most often it is cut crystal in a particular shape and style. Sometimes the glass is even photographed so that it can be replicated in the next place I visit. Then, my own mind becomes conditioned by habit. If I don't find a cut-crystal glass from the Czech Republic, my mind thinks, "I can't drink water from a paper cup. For Khandro Rinpoche, it should be crystal." We could choose to see and appreciate things for what they are. Water is water. Whether we drink from a crystal glass or cupped hands, it's about satisfying thirst. How we do it doesn't matter, but we are conditioned to think such things matter very much.

When everything is seen from a conditioned perspective, there is a lack of insight into things as they truly are. There is therefore an inability to recognize one's inherent nature. You can choose to change that perspective. In the search for teachings and truth, look to see if what you are searching for isn't something you already have. Look for it at home. Certainly no one is bringing anything from the East that does not already grow in the West.

If You Really Want Happiness

If you really want happiness, start from the basis of the inherent goodness within you and remain true to that. This is what it means to become an awakened one. Foremost in the life of any buddha is the potential for basic goodness at any moment in time. Instead, from morning to night, we human beings try very hard to create happiness for ourselves. We put so much effort into our families, relationships, money, and spiritual practices, all to obtain some comfort, contentment, and benefit. This is what the Buddha found to be true.

As a prince, the Buddha was very much loved by some people and very much hated by others—all of them trying to create happiness for themselves. His father and mother were trying to find happiness. The aunts and uncles who wanted him dead and the cousin who kept trying to kill him wanted happiness. The ministers who were for and against him were trying to find happiness. His wife was trying to find happiness. His own escape from the kingdom was in search of happiness. The Buddha realized that while we all want happiness, we don't really know how to go about getting it. We approach it in ways that are very different from who we are, intrinsically, by nature.

Imagine, for example, that you arrange a wonderful dinner for some friends you haven't seen in years. You invite them for a reunion so you can all catch up. The spread you create is wonderful, but unfortunately your behavior is neurotic. You become aggressive, negative, and you say hurtful things. All the effort you put into having a happy moment becomes a disaster—an experience of pain, suffering, and confusion for everyone. This is how we live our lives.

We all do want happiness; no one wants unhappiness. But we are unable to relate correctly with the happiness we hope for. Why is this? The reason is ignorance. We don't know what creates happiness and what prevents suffering. This is the realization that triggered the Buddha's search for the true cause of happiness and freedom from suffering. As a Buddhist practitioner, keep this realization deep in your mind and meditation.

What causes us to search for lasting happiness where it can never be found? How is it that, as much as we run from it, we are never really free of suffering? Before gaining realization, the Buddha sought answers to these questions from his teachers in the Hindu tradition.

At that time in India, two philosophies were prevalent. The one from the Vedic tradition believed in a pure everlasting soul, or *atman*, created by Brahma. If one were pure and truly adhered to the practices and teachings, one's own soul became Brahma's soul, a sort of ultimate pure self. The second strong belief was held by the Charvaka, a nihilist group popular among the warrior clans. Their philosophy was that we are made up of aggregates, and at the time of death, these aggregates dissolve into nothingness. Because we are simply born out of the coming together of elements, they were against any moralistic or ethical beliefs.

These two very popular beliefs did not satisfy the Buddha's need to understand the powerful pursuit of happiness that drives our existence. All that we do, say, think, build, create, or destroy is in search of happiness. And does any of it lead to the lasting freedom from suffering and pain that we're searching for? The answer is "No."

My teacher used to say, "Even at the height of your laughter, listen to the sound of discontent." This is the sound of the fear that our happiness is going to change. This anxiousness, restlessness, and discontent are what we must uncover and go beyond. How do we do that? Everything we study and learn, all the teachers we follow, and whatever changes we bring into our lives are in search of that answer—and like the Buddha, we may still find ourselves dissatisfied with the answers.

Meditation is the actual practice of the Buddha's teachings.

The Buddha found his answer in meditation. You may do other practices such as chanting, reciting mantras, and so on—this is all very good. But how often do you sit down and look at the restlessness and discontent related to your pursuit of happiness and freedom from suffering? How often do you ask yourself what you can do about that? If you do take the time to recognize what it is that's driving you to find answers, you are actually doing what the Buddha did.

But how often does the mind shift a bit, and you start thinking that if you just do some mantras, if you just sit in meditation like a good Buddhist, something will happen? This is a mind inclined to depend on something other than an awakening to the answer within you. This kind of mind is the demarcation between two groups of people: the faithful loyalists, as I call them, and true practitioners.

The loyalists make up a wonderful group of people who are loyal to Buddhist ideology. Then there are those who are truly practitioners. Loyalists are not true practitioners; and true practitioners don't care if they're loyal or not, as long as the true answer is recognized and realized. These are people who could be seen as Buddhists in the true sense of the word. This is what could be seen as true practice, in the sense of the Buddha, himself.

TWO

Three Basic Laws of Nature That Can't Be Ignored

BEYOND ALL THE imagined glamour of the Buddha's realization, what he truly understood were three simple things: impermanence, suffering, and no self. Known as the three marks of existence, called *anitya*, *duhkha*, and *anatman* in Sanskrit, they are the essential principles of the Buddha's teachings. Understanding them led to the Buddha's "great awakening"—words that are really too glamorous, as this was not an extravagant realization. The Buddha simply awakened to the truth of three basic laws of nature and the truth that not understanding them is the cause of suffering and struggle.

First, the Buddha awakened to the fact that everything changes. Because we don't want things to change, our tendency is to tighten our grip and try to solidify things, which doesn't allow for any natural ease, relaxation, or enjoyment in the present moment. So, the first thing that is not properly understood is impermanence. The second is suffering: the suffering caused by not understanding interdependence. Whether we call it interconnectedness or interdependent origination, the fact is that everything that comes into being is dependent on the coming together of a great many temporary causes and conditions—all of them changing and evolving.

This simple natural law may have been recognized by the learned ones of the time, but it wasn't given much importance with regard to the pursuit of happiness and freedom from suffering. The third thing the Buddha understood was that, ultimately, the true nature of things is empty. This emptiness nature is not a void, but it is also not a reality that we can hold on to or pin down. Our tendency to do so causes suffering and struggle. In the words of the great Mahamudra teachings of Buddhism, life's ongoing struggle is called karma.

SWIMMING AGAINST THE STREAM

Basically, we have been swimming against the strong current of natural law. This constant struggle with the truth of things as they are is called karma. This is what the Buddha's realization allowed him to see. Today the word *karma* can be found in most dictionaries and is widely used. But what does it really mean? Simply put, it refers to the relationship between actions and their consequences. But this interconnectedness is a very big picture. Just as a small fistful of seeds can ripen into a field of grain, small acts can have far reaching consequences, for better or worse. Moreover, there is individual and collective karma. How can this be? If there is no solid self, we are not just looking at our own lives with their ups and downs or the consequences of our actions and views. We are looking at vast world systems of karmic patterns, which like everything else are impermanent, empty by nature, and interdependent.

Thus, karma has nothing to do with judgment; there is no one above or below keeping track. Karma is simply the wholeness of all these causes and consequences, seeds and fruit. From this perspective, we can see the busyness and speed of karma and how karma can move us away from the truth of things as they are and into habitual struggles with the way they are not. While it would be nice if the struggle were about something brilliant, it is basically about three things: the struggle to make what is impermanent permanent, the struggle to turn the interconnectedness of things into separateness, and the struggle to solidify things that by nature are not solid. And so we go on building more houses, creating more relationships, and buying frying pans that are guaranteed to last for twenty years.

When the nuns and I went shopping for a frying pan recently, we were shown a pan made by Le Creuset, a company that makes good pots and pans. This pan has a guarantee of twenty years and a guarantee card to prove it. Now, this is hilarious because the frying pan will probably outlive me. But it was a nice thought and we chose that pan because it was guaranteed. This is how we struggle each day to prove that we can make what is impermanent permanent. This is the struggle to sustain a stubborn belief in independence, disregarding the fact that all things come into being through the interconnectedness of causes and conditions—which are, themselves, not permanent or solid.

CONTEMPLATION

Today many of our sangha members are aging. You observe every white hair on your head, every wrinkle, every pain in the knee or the back. But if you go to bed at night fed up and tired, you should ask yourself why you're so tired and fed up and in so much pain. What have you done to get yourself into this physical and emotional shape? You haven't done anything remarkable other than these three things: For the sake of convenience, you have been struggling to make the impermanent permanent. You have been struggling to make things that are interdependent independent. And you have been struggling to solidify things that inherently don't exist by labeling them with names that you would like everyone else to accept.

And Justifying That

When ego is involved, we are the last ones to admit that our struggle was really unnecessary. To make things worse, we justify the struggle, which is especially painful when there are no takers for our justifications. Add to that six or seven billion people, all insisting on justifying what they think to be permanent, what they think to be right, and what they think to be real—and we're bound to have disagreements in the world.

Why don't we just let go? We have immediate justifications for not doing so: "This is not about me; it's for the children, for posterity, and so on." We do things like creating practice centers, which get us into lots of issues that we could do without. But the struggle is sustained "to benefit generations to come." Who knows if it actually will? But this is our justification, like the justifications for buying another car, building another house, starting another relationship, finding another job, or saying something harsh.

Suffering comes with the constant struggle against the three basic laws of nature—impermanence, interdependence, and the emptiness nature of things—and then having to justify that. The Buddha witnessed this in his own life. His cousin thought, "If I could just kill the prince, I'd be happy." The king thought, "When my son becomes king, I'll be happy; if he does not, I'll be very unhappy." The Buddha began to see this constant struggle and justification of struggle as the first Noble Truth: the truth of suffering.

The origin of the Buddha's concept of suffering was not simply birth, old age, sickness, and death. That kind of suffering—like the suffering of violence, aggression, and other negativities—is easily identifiable. But then there is, even in the midst of our laughter, the subtle discontent consisting of the subtle wish to secure this moment and keep it safe and the fear that this moment will pass, never to come again.

A young couple once came to a retreat madly in love. Throughout the teachings they were whispering back and forth, "Do you love me?" and "You know I love you." Not long after that, they separated. When I asked the young woman what happened, she said, "He doesn't love me the way he did before." This is a good example of trying to make something impermanent into something permanent, by trying to repeat the same thing again and again.

Instead, you could allow things to change and evolve. You could release time from your demands and release others from your control. This is what compassion is about. Compassion releases others from your struggle to make them conform to your wishes. There is a great deal of kindness in giving others the freedom to evolve naturally as they are—and a lot of patience involved in that.

CONTEMPLATION

Recognizing that all human beings want to be happy and do not want to suffer, begin by examining these two things: struggle and the justification of struggle. Then you will understand the unnecessary suffering we put most of our energy into, all due to not understanding impermanence, interdependence, and the emptiness nature of things.

HOW THE BUDDHA CONVEYED HIS UNDERSTANDING

The Buddha's own understanding was born out of these three marks of existence. First, since everything is changing, accept change. Second, since everything is interdependent, work with the interconnectedness of things, allowing for the fact that all of life's experiences originate from interdependent causes and conditions. And third, see clearly that these causes and conditions themselves originate from emptiness—not emptiness as nothingness but emptiness as the beautiful ground that allows everything to come into being. This understanding was called the Buddha's great awakening.

How did the Buddha convey this understanding? He began by teaching what came to be known as the Four Noble Truths: suffering, the cause of suffering, the cessation of suffering, and the path. The truth of suffering is struggle, the bottom-line struggle being the attempt to see things that are inherently impermanent, interdependent, and empty as if they were permanent, separate, and solid.

The cause of this suffering is called ignorance. The Tibetan term for ignorance is *marigpa*, which means "not knowing the true nature of things." So ignorance here is not just one big blob. Ignorance is the subtle layers of assumptions upon which we base our confused view of the world. With the grace and generosity to go beyond our assumptions, beyond appearances and sensory convenience, we can know the truth of things as they really are. With this discovery comes the cessation of suffering and struggle. This is the ground of the Buddha's path.

AN EIGHTFOLD PATH OF PRACTICE

Essentially, you could say that the practice of Buddhism is nothing other than eight principles, best known as the eightfold path. These eight principles are right view, right thought, right speech, right action, right livelihood, right effort, right mindfulness, and right concentration.

Right View

Knowing that ignorance is the cause of suffering and struggle with all its justifications, we would first want to free ourselves from ignorance. For this, we would cultivate the right view. What would the right view be for a Buddhist? Right view is based on an understanding of how and why we are caught in this cyclic existence. It is based on seeing the immense restlessness of a mind wanting to attain happiness and avoid suffering. This raises a question: How and why would a human being who is endowed with brilliant potential and all good qualities be unable to remain true to those qualities? It is a strange situation.

MIND'S TWELVE PROGRESSIVE STEPS

Right view means understanding how this restless mind functions in twelve progressive steps, or stages, called *nidanas*. Like the cycle of life itself—with its stages of birth, living, dying, death, and rebirth—the nidanas can be seen as twelve interdependent links of origination. These links describe how we constantly move the mind outward. From a practice perspective, they can be seen to take place at every moment.

The first stage is a moment of unawareness, or ignorance. But again, the word *ignorance* seems very heavy-duty, visually like a big lump, whereas *marigpa* means "to not see clearly." This is beautifully described as a moment of stupefaction—like the first moment you look in the mirror after a makeover, you are stupefied. The mind becomes very vivid, with all its senses busily perceiving and projecting thoughts and feelings. Getting caught up in this vividness, we become unaware of our innate true nature and more aware of something else. This state of unawareness is called *ignorance*.

The second stage is formation. From unawareness something begins to take shape. We may not even know what it is. Some energy just catches our attention, like a glass dropped on a tile floor. Before we can even decipher what happened, our attention is concentrated outward. That is the second stage: formation. The third stage is called *consciousness*. Stupefied by the mind's response to the previous moment, consciousness becomes a biased sort of energy, which immediately gives birth to the fourth stage. The fourth stage is name and form. Whatever catches our attention, even a word or an idea, is given a name and form. When we hear the word *ugly*, for example, we think we know what it is. When we hear *beautiful*, without even knowing what is beautiful, an idea or mental image begins to form. This embellishing is name and form. A name is just a label, but we have a habit of solidifying labels and giving them characteristics. In this way, struck by its own vividness, the mind moves from formation to consciousness to a name and some definite form—at which point the six senses begin to function.

The fifth stage consists of the six senses. The five physical senses include the ability to see, hear, smell, taste, and have tactile sensations; and the sixth sense is consciousness, the mind that begins to have some idea of what we're talking about. When the senses come into contact with names and forms—visual forms, forms of thought and sound, and so on—this is the sixth stage, or link, called contact. From sensory contact arises the seventh link, feeling. This stage refers to the inevitable feelings that arise from contact. Feelings—good, bad, or indifferent—enhance the subsequent links, beginning with the eighth stage, craving.

Habitual craving simply wants something deeply. At this point, we usually delve into familiar old feelings and memories and become very involved in continuing to like what we like and dislike what we dislike. We then crave those familiar feelings. With heightened craving there is grasping, which is the ninth stage. The moment of grasping onto something leads the mind into the tenth stage, becoming. This is followed by the eleventh stage, birth, which is followed by the twelfth stage, death.

These twelve stages, or links, happen in a flash in every moment. If I hear a glass drop on the floor, I think, "What happened?" And immediately I delve into past memories: glass, fell, crashed, not good. I then know exactly what to say: "Too bad. Shall I get a mop?" Such reflexive responses happen constantly.

In Buddhist mindfulness meditation, one would observe this pattern again and again. Why would one do that? At every moment, we could rest in our own awake nature instead of moving into the habitual energy of formation and the consciousness that gives rise to names, forms, biases, grasping, and so on. But our immense familiarity with habitually creating those twelve outer links causes the struggles and justifications to begin to spin. And in this way, karmic causes are created. Like drops of water filling a vessel, karmic causes become the basis for our future experiences.

The spinning of the twelve links creates the cycle of suffering called *samsara*. Reversing the cycle of samsara is the basis of Buddhist meditation. Sitting still, in silence, and reducing activity and distractions are what allow you to cut through the habitual twelve links. By reversing the process of constantly looking outward, you become more familiar with looking within. These considerations have to do with right view, the first stage of the eightfold path. The second step is right thought.

Right Thought

Right thought is very simple. If you want happiness, cultivate good thoughts: thoughts filled with an understanding of others, with patience, generosity, kindness, and love.

Right Speech

To cultivate good speech, look to see what your speech produces. What karmic causes do you create with lying, slander, gossip, or harsh words? If you want happiness, speak gently or not at all. If you must speak, say something nice. This is the third step.

Right Action

Right action is the path of practice. As a human being who truly wants happiness, mentally watch the actions of your mind. Generate the kind of good thoughts and good speech that become good actions. This physically creates good karmic causes, or seeds—good in the truest sense. This brings us to the fifth step, right livelihood.

Right Livelihood

The Buddha never spoke about not earning a living. It is a misunderstanding to think you have to give up your job or occupation to be a Buddhist. Right livelihood simply means that your livelihood should not cause harm. Specifically, this means that your livelihood is not based upon three main things: deceit; any kind of anger, harshness, or harm to others; and hypocrisy. As long as you are not earning your living through deceit, harming others, or hypocrisy, any kind of livelihood is acceptable. Just keep in mind that in order to transform your thoughts, speech, and actions into right thought, right speech, and right action, the work you do must be based on right livelihood.

Right Effort

Right effort refers to consistently putting your effort into the four kinds of right action:

1. Making an effort to be ethical so that your every action produces virtue.

2. Making an effort to increase the virtues you have and to generate those that are absent. For example, if you are honest but also impatient, make an effort to develop patience as well.

3. Making an effort to ensure there are no unvirtuous actions of body, speech, or mind. This refers specifically to ten unvirtuous actions: three of body (killing, stealing, and sexual misconduct); four of speech (lying, sowing discord, harsh abusive speech, and frivolous idle chatter); and three of mind (wishing harm to others, covetousness, and wrong views).

4. Making an effort to eliminate any nonvirtue in your attitude and conduct.

Right Mindfulness

Right mindfulness gathers together all of the above. You are observant and watchful of whatever you think, say, or physically engage in. What is your true intention or motivation in these activities? What is your perspective? If you truly want happiness, are you creating positive causes and abstaining from negative, unvirtuous actions? Right mindfulness brings about the wisdom of discrimination, which discerns and eliminates harmful causes and produces positive causes.

Right Concentration

The eighth aspect of the path is right concentration. You are watchful and mindful in all activities while deep down your mind is concentrated on its own true nature and ever-present potential for great goodness. When you wake up in the morning, this should be your first thought.

We can always choose to be true to our potential to be nothing but good in the truest sense of the word. At any point in the day, we have that choice because this is our inherent true nature. Of course, distractions are many, and we don't always remain true to our potential. As a parent, you might wave your finger at a child and say, "Be true to yourself. You can be good. You can be the best." But how often do we say this to ourselves? Teach yourself to concentrate on your potential to be nothing but good the same way you would teach a young child. This is right concentration, the eighth aspect of the eightfold path.

THE ESSENCE OF ANY PRACTICE YOU DO

The essence of any practice you do—any visualization or mantra, any form or formless meditation, Buddhist or non-Buddhist—is the inherent true nature of your mind. This is your true potential. Whether you call it basic goodness, buddha nature, enlightenment, or absolute truth, this is what you should be true to. This simple truth is often made unnecessarily difficult and complex because this is our human habit.

On one hand, there is ignorance and all the causes of unhappiness and negative karma that we create. On the other hand, there is the realization we aspire to and all the virtue and goodness we create. The line between them is very thin. At every moment, you can be inclined this way or that. The choice is yours. The only thing that inclines you toward confusion, suffering, and the creation of samsara is your familiarity with it. This is what you are used to. Like any reflexive response, it happens automatically and doesn't require any time or concentration. Nevertheless, you can always choose to be true to your basic nature. You can always choose to hold this as your view.

It is because we have the choice—and because we're so unfamiliar with making this choice—that the Buddhist path and commitment to meditation evolved. Out of necessity, starting with the Buddha, teachers had to come up with ways of saying, "Sit still. Be quiet. Don't be distracted. Watch your breath. Relax your mind." Why else would great enlightened beings be interested in putting you into various postures or having you breathe this way or that?

Do you have to be a Buddhist to awaken in this way? Definitely not! The problem is, we human beings are habituated to not responding to our true goodness. How do we become more responsive? Out of necessity, the Buddhist teachings, path, and sense of ethics evolved.

Ethics from This Point of View

Buddhist ethics is about being conscious of karma, conscious of virtuous actions, and conscious of earning merit.

The logic of Buddhist ethics does not have to do with any religious belief. It has nothing to do with pacifying deities; it doesn't even have to do with the Buddha. When you die, there is no one taking note of your past actions to determine whether you go to heaven or hell. Buddhist ethics is about being conscious of karma, conscious of virtuous actions, and conscious of earning merit.

With an understanding of how karma works in our lives, ten virtuous actions came to be seen as the basis of Buddhist ethics and the eightfold path. In practice, the ten virtuous actions refer to simply abandoning the ten unvirtuous actions, or causes of suffering—keeping in mind that the root cause of suffering is the self-cherishing from which these unvirtuous actions arise.

There are three unvirtuous actions of body (killing, stealing, and sexual misconduct); four unvirtuous actions of speech (lying, sowing discord, harsh abusive speech, and frivolous idle chatter); and three unvirtuous actions of mind (wishing harm to others, covetousness, and wrong views). From this point of view, the virtuous actions of body are to save and protect lives, to be generous, and to be sexually honorable. Virtuous speech is truthful, harmonious, gentle, and meaningful. And the virtuous actions of mind are the cultivation of contentment, or non-grasping; the cultivation of loving kindness; and the cultivation of a right, or selfless, view.

The actual benefit of abandoning unvirtuous acts and cultivating virtuous acts is called merit. Merit, in short, is our confidence in a way of being beyond self-cherishing. From the first glimmer of understanding that letting go of the self is not a tragedy—that it actually brings relaxation, joy, and happiness—there is merit. With the gathering of merit, wisdom spontaneously arises. This is the logic to apply to the mind whose outward momentum is so stuck in habitual ways of looking at things, it never sees things as they are.

The logic is simple. Let's say you complain that you have no friends, no one likes you, no one talks to you. The moment you walk into a room, however, you have a habit of saying hurtful things, like "What kind of hair cut is that?" or "That's a terrible color on you." This habit is unlikely to make you many friends or bring you much happiness. Thus, someone who wants happiness and does not want suffering foolishly creates endless causes for the very opposite of their wishes.

If we speak of the preciousness of human life and its creative potential, how willing are we to put this into practice?

As intelligent, thinking people, we all have something to complain about, don't we? The government, the environment, political leaders, religious leaders—we express our concerns about every negative occurrence. In this way, we constantly move away from the potential for good, and we do the very thing we're complaining about. If we speak of the preciousness of human life and its creative potential, how willing are we to put this into practice? If we have spent decades wanting happiness, peace, and contentment, how committed are we to planting the actual causes, or seeds, of that aspiration?

Buddhist logic says that if you plant a lemon seed and pray for a mango fruit, logically it won't work. Likewise, wishing for happiness without planting the seeds of happiness won't work. With some understanding of what the true seeds of happiness and suffering are, who then is responsible if the situations facing the world today are mean-spirited and violent? If society is unstable and unfriendly, we are all contributing to it. If the environment is suffering, we are all contributing. Individually, our contributions may not seem like much, but from a Buddhist perspective, what we're doing may be irresponsible. It is essential to understand this human behavior. From the comfort of self-cherishing habits of mind come our attitudes, judgments, character, behavior—and pain.

The only way to reverse this process is to cultivate right view, right thought, right speech, right action, right livelihood, right effort, right mindfulness, and right concentration.

Because You're a Human Being

We have seen how the Buddha came to understand three basic things: impermanence, interdependence, and the core emptiness nature of things. Not understanding this, we create struggle and the exhausting justification of struggle. Being oblivious to this, we create karma and the causes of suffering. This gives us some idea why anyone might adopt a Buddhist view or path of practice: it is not out of loyalty to certain ideas but is based on seeing how things naturally evolve and what they become.

Seeing this, you might begin to practice in order to eradicate the problem. You don't practice because you're a Buddhist, but rather you practice to diminish the ignorant belief in permanence, separateness, and the solidity of things, which we habitually see more clearly than things as they naturally are. To sustain this shift in perspective, you might rely on the support of a path of practice. And if you work with right view, right thought, right speech, right action, right livelihood, right effort, right mindfulness, and right concentration in your everyday life, you might call yourself a Buddhist practitioner.

If you believe yourself to be a Buddhist—practice the eightfold path! If your practice includes the recitation of mantras, very good. If you sit in meditation, do it. But always imbue whatever you do with the eightfold path. Without the eightfold path in your life, you could not be called a true Buddhist. And if you call yourself a non-Buddhist, the eightfold path is absolutely necessary, simply because you are a human being.

All human beings have the potential for nothing but genuine goodness at every moment. If you so choose, the next moment you step into could be the ground of nothing but happiness for yourself and others. If you could sustain that without there being anything Buddhist about it, perfect! That's being a non-Buddhist in the best sense. But if you were honest with yourself, you might think, "Yes, I can do this. But to sustain it, it might be good to have some kind of reminder or structure or support."

It is for this reason—throughout all the various cultures and traditions—that the different methods of practice evolved. In order to allow one to go more deeply into the discovery of one's basic goodness, some traditions believe in keeping things as formless as possible. Other traditions believe that the human mind and neurotic habits are so complex that they call for even more complicated and complex methods. Ultimately, it is like "catching hold of your nose," as we Tibetans like to say. It doesn't matter which way you catch hold of your nose, this way or that. Just catch it!

CONTEMPLATION

The wisdom in understanding the cause of suffering is in knowing you can come out of it. You can actually eradicate the cause of suffering.

How do you do that? You do it by shifting your perspective. With an understanding of how the human mind works, instead of taking your mind outward into habitual distractions, look inward. This is what is meant by right view. To cultivate right thought, be kind. To cultivate right speech, be kind. To cultivate right action and right livelihood, be kind. To cultivate right effort, always be kind. Be mindful and kind, and be concentrated and kind. This is what it means to be a good Buddhist.

THREE

The Buddha's Definition
of Social Responsibility

DURING THE TIME the Buddha was turning the wheel of Dharma in India, his enlightened wisdom became renowned. A well-known Hindu sage had become curious about the Buddha's teachings and longed to understand in his own mind what the Buddha had realized. But with thousands of followers of his own, he was bound by responsibilities and was never able to approach the Buddha directly.

During one of his journeys, however, he chanced upon a Buddhist monk, whose radiance and serenity struck him. Discovering that this exceptional monk was a student of the Buddha, the sage asked,

"What does your teacher teach?" Taken aback by the question, the monk replied, "It would be impossible to summarize the enlightened teachings of the Buddha, the great Muni, the Tathagatha. But if I were to put into a simple verse what I think the Buddha teaches, it would be this:

Do nothing unvirtuous.
Do everything that is virtuous.

Train your mind.
This is Buddhadharma.

Because the sage was exceptionally learned and realized, he immediately captured the pith as well as the enormity of these four lines. Most importantly, he saw clearly the intent of the Buddha and his teachings: it was never to create another religion. Struck by the truth of what the Buddha was teaching, this master went back to his students and said, "I am going to take refuge with the Buddha. Those who wish to join me can join me. Those who do not wish to join me can continue practicing as I have taught you." Then, based on those three profound lines, the sage went off and became the Buddha's disciple.

Historically, these simple lines are significant because they were uttered by Shariputra, one of the Buddha's main students, to the sage who became known as Mahakashyapa. When the Buddha passed away, it was Mahakashyapa who became the Buddha's successor and heir to his teachings. Moreover, in these four lines, the three turnings of the wheel of Dharma and the teachings of the three yanas—Hinayana, Mahayana, and Vajrayana—are beautifully condensed.

DO NOTHING UNVIRTUOUS

The key to understanding the nature of mind—enlightenment, absolute truth, call it what you will—lies in understanding these ten basic unvirtuous activities.

The first of Shariputra's lines says to not do anything unvirtuous. The Tibetan word for "unvirtuous," *digpa*, might be described like this: You go up onto the roof of the temple, where you find some large object that weighs about a ton. You push it to the edge of the roof and wait for someone to pass by. Then you topple this one-ton object onto their head. What happens to the person on the ground? They are crushed. This is what digpa, or unvirtuous action, does. It crushes whomever it encounters. It drags you down and pulls you away from your innate potential. There are many ways to crush someone. There is verbal crushing, emotional crushing, and the crushing of all hopes and dreams, inspiration, abilities, qualities, or potential. To engage in any physical, verbal, or mental action that has the power to crush another is unvirtuous.

Historically in Tibet, the notion of unvirtuous action was introduced as the ten unvirtuous acts mentioned above: the three unvirtuous actions of body, four of speech, and three of mind. When I began studying Buddhism, our teachers always wanted to make very sure we understood which ten unvirtuous activities to abandon. We, on the other hand, always wanted to hurry on to the profound teachings, like the true nature of mind. But the key to understanding the nature of mind—enlightenment, absolute truth, call it what you will—lies in understanding these ten basic unvirtuous activities.

At first glance, we all assume that we don't go around killing, stealing, or indulging in sexual misconduct, and so on. But if we examine our actions more closely, we might find we kill and lie all the time. And if we don't openly indulge in sexual misconduct, who knows what goes on in our minds? A human being in search of enlightenment should at least be aware that the life of another is as precious as their own. But how many animals and other sentient beings had to give up their lives to enable this human body to survive? One way or another, we harm sentient beings with every physical act. Likewise, while we may not break into houses to steal, we definitely take things that don't belong to us.

The unvirtuous acts of speech and mind are more evasive and well hidden. But can you honestly say you don't lie, gossip, speak harsh or angry words, slander, criticize, or express ill will toward anyone?

Without any religious or spiritual connotations, these fundamental disciplines are considered part of our human nature: simple things that we teach to our children. Why then, with all our good qualities and acquired knowledge, can this human mind not abandon actions that are universally known to be negative, harmful, and useless? Failing that, how could one understand absolute truth, develop selflessness, or let go of all attachment?

Knowing what it means to abandon unvirtuous actions
was the Buddha's definition of social responsibility—not
because you're a Buddhist but because you are a human
being.

A basic Buddhist principle says, "Just as I want happiness, all sentient beings want happiness. Just as I don't want pain and suffering, no sentient being wants pain and suffering." If the actions of this physical body, speech, and mind are not respectful of life, how could this mind be called a "human" mind or realize something as valuable as enlightenment or freedom from suffering? Anyone on a spiritual path—any spiritual path—needs to consider this question.

Shariputra's first line is the basis of the Hinayana teachings. It is useful to know that when the first Buddhist scholars and teachers were invited from India by the kings of Tibet, they did not immediately teach the many great Mahayana teachings or the profound Vajrayana teachings. They taught the basic Hinayana practices having to do with an awareness of morality, or self-discipline. Through awareness, discipline, and the ability to discern what is harmful, one abandons useless, harmful activities.

At that time, Tibet was considered to be a barbarian country. This didn't mean that Tibetans were barbarous in the ordinary sense. They were intelligent human beings who simply didn't give themselves the time and space to do things in accord with their basic human potential. Caring only for one's own survival and thinking only of oneself—even animals can do this. Yet we human beings view ourselves as the most intelligent of all species. What is it, then, that human beings can do beyond surviving and protecting ourselves? We can fully realize our human potential.

To this end, the first teachings brought into Tibet were the Hinayana teachings on abandoning the ten unvirtuous acts. Later, during the reign of King Songtsen Gampo, they would serve as the basis of Tibet's first constitution. But it would be a misunderstanding to view the abandoning of unvirtuous actions as dogma. It is essential to know what it means experientially.

Knowing what it means to abandon unvirtuous actions was the Buddha's definition of social responsibility—not because you're a Buddhist but because you are a human being. Then you would understand what the Buddha was saying in so few words: Do nothing unvirtuous.

DO EVERYTHING THAT IS VIRTUOUS

Essentially, there is no defining characteristic of virtue. Saying something "good" might be unvirtuous if it is said for your own benefit; saying something harsh might be virtuous. Saying something harsh could be the greatest blessing you could give someone; on the other hand, you could be killing them with kindness. The bottom line is this: Nonvirtue is whatever really crushes another. Virtue is the courage to go beyond the self-indulgent mind.

In English, the word *virtue* often has to do with morality, with being spiritually or morally good. Whereas the Tibetan word for "virtue," *gewa*, has a sense of an inner capability. Since the innate nature of a human being is pure, *gewa* points to the ability to leap from a state of ignorance, or impurity, to a state of innate purity in body, speech, and mind. Simply put, *virtue* means the capability to go beyond what is easy and convenient for the self.

For example, if you volunteer to help out with some everyday situation, I might ask how much you can do—optimistically, pessimistically, or realistically. Due to the optimistic or pessimistic boundaries you set for yourself, you will gauge your limitations and apply vague conditions to whatever you do. It's like a prenuptial contract. Your capabilities have terms and conditions: How generous can I be? How kind or patient can I be?

Let's say someone asks if you want to go for a walk. Watch how your mind immediately sets limitations: "Well, I don't want to walk to the top of the mountain" or "Okay, I'll walk halfway there and back." If there's a reason to go into town, you might say, "I'll go if you go." Who imposes these conditions and boundaries? This reflexive momentum is bounded by some vague sense of self.

Thus our physical actions, our speech, and especially our ideas, emotions, and thoughts are constantly conditioned by the dictates of self-absorption. We may think we know about the self and its nature, but we may underestimate its power to dictate the parameters of our every thought, word, and action. Virtue recognizes that these limitations and conditions—which may not even be reasonable or meaningful— are the reason we cannot interact sanely with one another. To culti- vate virtue means to free oneself from self-cherishing limitations and conditions. This is the focus of Shariputra's second line.

This second line is the basis of the Mahayana teachings on the path of transformation known as the bodhisattva path. Ultimately, *gewa*, or "virtue," is the confidence you have in your own basically good nature. At this stage, not only are you better able to avoid harming others, you are better able to help them. Having developed self-discipline and extended this toward others, you can tap into helpful qualities that might actually be of some use to the world. Free from self-absorbed agendas and boundaries, you are totally available to whatever situation you face. This is what it means to "do everything that is virtuous."

Virtuous action requires spontaneity, naturalness, absolute hon- esty, wakefulness, and a fair degree of flexibility. It evolves in re- sponse to whatever is needed, not just to what's easy. This is the meaning of the bodhisattva path.

TRAIN YOUR MIND

The history of Buddhism began with these profound fundamental instructions of Shakyamuni Buddha, and they are still of benefit today. It doesn't matter whether you consider yourself a spiritual or unspiritual person or a Mahayana, Vajrayana, Dzogchen, or Ma- hamudra Buddhist. The only thing that matters is to avoid the ten unvirtuous actions and put the ten virtuous actions into practice. This, however, is easy to talk about and difficult to do.

To abandon nonvirtue and accomplish virtue you must train your own—not someone else's—mind. This is the focus of Shariputra's third line, which is the only way to accomplish the preceding two lines. To train this stubborn, stubborn mind, there is a vast array of methods and skillful means, all of them meant to free one from attachment to a "self" for the benefit of oneself and others.

The extraordinary skillful means of the Vajrayana then develop the ongoing awareness that spontaneously transcends self-cherishing. With the collapse of falsity, the true nature of mind is revealed and genuine compassion can spontaneously arise. This is the basis of the Vajrayana, which is the focus of Shariputra's third line.

THIS IS BUDDHADHARMA

Thus in three simple lines, the meaning and pith instructions of the three yanas of the Buddhist teachings are contained.

Shariputra's fourth line, "This is Buddhadharma," not only contains the quintessence of the previous lines, it also reveals the Buddha's intent. Out of compassion, Shakyamuni Buddha expounded eighty-four thousand teachings during his time on earth. Today, twenty-five hundred years later, the Buddhist teachings are so vast, it would be difficult to comprehend them all within a human lifetime. Yet all of these teachings are gathered into these three simple lines of instruction, which point to a deep sense of kindness and a recognition of one's own true nature.

THE PRACTICE OF KINDNESS

With the growing awareness of Buddhist teachings and culture, it is essential that we also grow in a good way. Healthy growth is based on kindness, patience, and not losing touch with our basic sanity and intelligence. From a simple humanitarian point of view, kindness is necessary. For someone who has met with the Dharma, the practice of kindness is essential.

CONTEMPLATION

Kindness, in the end, depends on virtue. Virtue comes down to good actions of body, good actions of speech, and good actions of mind in the form of positive thoughts.

Our actions are causes of consequences, good or bad. For as long as you have a body and mind, always discern clearly whether the actions of your body, speech, and mind may be harmful. Abandon harmful actions, and cultivate conduct that is helpful and a cause of happiness for yourself and others. One who genuinely develops such awareness is a true Buddhist practitioner, even without the label.

Not External Solutions, Convenience, or Corruption

When Mahakashyapa heard Shariputra summarize in four lines what the Buddha taught, he had an extraordinary understanding of the Buddha's call to human beings to develop their intrinsic mind. Coming from the Hindu tradition, he saw it was not about becoming a "Buddhist"; there was no need for such external changes. For any human being, this shift in perspective would bring about the most extraordinary change.

If Buddhism were just another doctrine, philosophy, or religion, it was not at all needed. Not only in India, but also throughout the world, there was no need for one more philosophy or religion. The Buddha's dissatisfaction was not with a particular religion or philosophy. It was with the way human beings locate their solution to happiness and unhappiness externally.

Moreover, he found that extreme reliance on something outside of oneself creates corruption: corruption of the individual, corruption of society, and therefore corruption of spirituality as well. Having an extrinsic sense of spirituality, however profound, becomes very convenient, and convenience makes for corruption. Here is a simple example: a student might offer a spiritual teacher a white silk *khatag* scarf and an envelope of money while thinking, "This will take care of my problems." Instead of relying on our intrinsic awareness and the training of our mind, we assume that all negative karma can be remedied externally, all problems solved easily and conveniently.

Such an approach leads to the corruption of our understanding of the Buddhist teachings—and this approach is seductive because it's so easy. Neither the teacher nor the student may have any idea what happens next, but like a waltz or a tango, they move about synchronizing their steps. That is the beautiful dance we can get into with Dharma and religion. We might be doing that same kind of dance when we light candles, offer flowers, do prostrations, or recite prayers. While such actions may be meritorious in and of themselves, whatever the motivation, we might still be missing the essential point. The Buddha was never satisfied with reliance on this kind of externalized relationship to religion.

The problem was never religion; none is better or worse than another. If you were to actually fully embody any religion, fully internalizing the philosophy without being seduced by corruption, there would be no need for the Buddha's teachings. Every religion is exceptional, every religion is sufficient—but along come human beings, with their human tendency to prioritize the convenience of the self before the true meaning.

> For the Buddha, it was never about just hearing teachings, it was about examining the teachings he was hearing.

The young Buddha's dissatisfaction was not so much with the Hindu teachings; it was with the human beings' response to that wonderful wisdom. It was at that point that his search became internal rather than external. For the Buddha, it was never about just hearing teachings, it was about examining the teachings he was hearing. This distinction has to be understood.

When Mahakashyapa heard the four-line verse, he understood that the Buddha was trying to awaken every human being to the intrinsic responsibility of having a human life. This is what inspired him to go and take refuge with the Buddha.

Keep that clear understanding of the Buddha's intent vividly in your awareness. This should be your own intention for putting these teachings into practice. If you are not clear about that, you will not become a practitioner of Dharma—you will become a "Buddhist"!

BECAUSE WE ARE INTERDEPENDENT

Given the interconnectedness of our lives, it is immensely important to become aware of the responsibility we share for one another.

The intent of the Buddha and the teachings known as Buddhadharma is poignantly, directly, and profoundly connected with our human lives and responsibility as human beings. This responsibility comes not only because we have a life, but also because our lives are interconnected. This truth, called "interdependent origination," is central to the Buddhist teachings and the Buddha's intent: that one with the most freedom, equipped with the most potential and qualities, be the first to awaken to the responsibility of interdependence.

It is because we are interdependent that we are responsible for developing our intrinsic mind. Now, if you were the only person in the world, this sense of responsibility might be more relaxed. You might take the occasional break from virtue and nonvirtue. Instead, we are all living together in an immensely complex network of interdependence, relying on one another for everything we do.

Given our interconnectedness, it is essential to overcome the myth of separateness and to wake up to the responsibility we share for one another. Truly realizing this generates a sense of empathy and ethics. It brings awareness of how our human choices generate health and harmony—or not—within our families, societies, and the environment as a whole. Theoretically, the logic is clear. Ideally, we would cultivate this understanding and put it into practice.

Practically speaking, however, we meet with an obstacle. The obstacle is ignorance. Ignorance imagines that individuals are not interdependent; it perpetuates the myth of separateness. And with six or seven billion human beings whose chief concern is the comfort and convenience of a separate self, living together on a densely populated planet, how could that not be a problem?

The Buddha's intent was about recognizing the fundamental social responsibility of a human being, whose life is interconnected with the lives of others. If, while trying to understand the Buddhist teachings, you and I fail to understand this intent, we will fail to understand why we do the things we do. The Buddha taught the Dharma so that the teachings awaken our stubborn minds to our responsibilities as human beings living on this planet.

It is crucial to recognize that the Buddha's intent, as taught through the three yanas, is to awaken within each of us the concept of interdependence. Awakening to this, all three stages of understanding speak to the importance of training one's mind, beginning with understanding our interconnectedness.

In a World of Constant Movement

If all sentient beings are interconnected, what is it that binds us? What do we have in common? In English, the binding factor is called *sentience*. All beings have sensory consciousness, thus the generic term *sentient beings*. But this is not how it is explained in the Buddhist texts. In Tibetan, the word "sentient" is just half of the term *drowa semchen*, where *drowa* means "movement" or simply "movers."

The one thing shared by all beings, from the tiniest bug to those we call human beings, is incessant movement—which is also known as cyclic existence, or *samsara*. Constant movement propels what we call our world.

Just because movement may not be visible to the naked eye does not mean a tremendous amount of movement is not taking place. Within thirty seconds, time-lapse photography can show a seed becoming a beautiful, full-grown tree. Now imagine looking at a thirty-second, time-lapse transformation of your own face from the time you were born. The physical movement of change would be visible. Likewise, there is the movement of the world's speech. If you could hear all the sounds made by all beings at this very moment, it would be deafening. And even when the body and speech are not moving, the mind is always moving. Reflect on the mental movements, feelings, and sensations of all sentient being at this very moment. To become even somewhat aware of this incessant movement would be enough to make you dizzy.

Over time, we have become so habituated to this movement that we never challenge it. We've developed the wonderful art of living in a cocoon, pretending we do not see the movement, do not hear the movement, and do not see that mind is constantly moving. This is the cocoon of ignorance. By sustaining this ignorance, the otherwise exceptional hearts and minds of human beings become apathetic, unfeeling, and uncaring.

This unsympathetic attitude refuses to understand the movement that is actually happening—and actually connecting all sentient beings.

CONTEMPLATION

To understand the interconnectedness of sentient beings, take time to get a sense of the tremendous movement of all aspects of life. Observe—within you and all around you—the physical movement, mental movement, and the movement of sound. This will give you some sense of the ceaseless movement throughout this world and all worldly existence.

Choosing How to Move through Life

The millions and billions of beings engaged in constant movement—physically, verbally, and mentally—are not moving "just because." As the teachings state, their movement is propelled by the search for happiness.

All beings want happiness, and we are not talking about just one big happiness. When you have an itch, for example, you find happiness in scratching it. When you shift in your seat, this movement is also a search for happiness. So often, the happiness we think we're looking for is actually just a pacification of the senses or momentary contentment. I once watched a documentary about a Zen hospice center in California. The director was speaking of his experience of what gives comfort and happiness to patients who are about to die. Number one on the list was the smell of fresh-baked cookies, especially for those who could no longer eat. In this case, just the smell of cookies can move the mind toward the possibility of happiness.

We sentient beings are propelled into movement by the thought that something we see, hear, smell, taste, feel, or imagine will give us happiness. What kind of happiness? Most often we don't know, exactly. It's elusive—but exciting enough to get us up and moving each day. The Buddha's intent was to awaken us to this incessant movement in search of happiness, to the complex network of interconnectedness it creates, and to the responsibility we have by virtue of being part of it.

Generally, the teachings describe two kinds of movement. The first is movement without choice, like the movement of a dry leaf in the wind. The second is movement with choice. Throughout the world, those with more freedom of choice are always considered to be more fortunate. In the Buddhist teachings, the most precious form of existence is said to be a human birth, for no other reason than the amount of freedom of choice we enjoy in our movement.

Yes, like all sentient beings, we suffer from the continuous movement propelled by habit and the search for happiness. But we also enjoy the greatest freedom to choose how and when we move or whether we move at all. By actively engaging in movements of your choosing, you can design how you move through your life, keeping in mind that the choices you make and the way you choreograph your movements create karma. As a human being, it falls to you to be fully responsible for the karma you create. The Buddha's teachings on abandoning negative karma and accumulating virtuous karma speak to this responsibility.

The Buddha's teachings on patience, generosity, and love are not meant for Buddhists alone. They address our responsibility as human beings. Since human beings have the greatest freedom to choose how they move, responsible human beings must ensure that the actions they create are virtuous. Virtue here is not so much a dictum or dogma as it is a call to human responsibility.

WHO HAS GREATER RESPONSIBILITY?

All sentient beings are in the same boat, propelled by a search for happiness. But some beings journeying across the ocean of samsara have more freedom of choice than others. All sentient beings—even animals such as cats, dogs, or pigs—create movement. But how much freedom of choice do they have in their movement? Between a human being and an animal, therefore, who do you think has greater responsibility?

Once, when we were preparing for a ceremony in India, a stray dog entered the temple and began eating a torma, a ritual cake made of dough. And before anyone could stop him, a monk picked up his shoe and hit the dog—at which point, everyone jumped on the monk. The point here is simple. The dog eating the torma created a movement that he thought would lead him to happiness. Likewise, the monk whacking the dog also created a movement in search of happiness. Between the two, who do you think could exercise more control over their choice of movement? Who had more responsibility to bring greater awareness to those actions?

Being the Eldest

We human beings are like the eldest in the family. I am the eldest in my family, with only one younger sister but more than forty cousins on my mother's side of the family. Even when I was young, I was told, "You're the eldest." I never liked hearing this because I would always be told "You're the eldest" when it came to sharing, being patient, or quieting down. When it came to losing an argument, I'd hear "It's okay, you're the eldest." But it is true, as the eldest how could I quarrel with my young cousins? What if a fifty-year-old Khandro Rinpoche were found outside fighting with a three-year-old over a piece of chocolate?

As a human being, you are the eldest in terms of your freedom of choice. It is simply your responsibility to be good, generous, kind, content, and a source of happiness for yourself and everyone connected to you. This is not because you are a Buddhist but because you know better. Whether or not you choose to enhance that knowing with the wisdom of the Dharma, this is how virtue should be seen.

To understand virtuous action, reflect on the ten unvirtuous actions and the constant habitual movement that keeps us from waking up to our interconnectedness and human responsibility. Movement and the need to move are very seductive, like an itch. But just as scratching an itch could actually cause a wound—and therefore more pain instead of relief—our movements in pursuit of what we assume to be happiness can actually cause more suffering. When, for example, something seems to threaten our pursuit of happiness, quicker than a flash of lightning, that sense of threat can cause us to respond in one of two ways. We contract or we react. Feeling threatened, we may contract within ourselves, becoming introverted and disassociated from others. On the other hand, we may be quick to react mentally, if not physically striking out—physical reactions being slower than our much faster mental reactions.

CONTEMPLATION

Reflect on the constant movement of billions of sentient beings, all propelled by the search for happiness and all sensitized to every threat. Observe this in your day-to-day life. Watch how you contract or react in response to any threat to your happiness. When this response becomes a habit, it is usually characterized by an attitude that is guarded or hostile. It is important to recognize the hostility and over-guardedness in your own attitude and movements.

What Does It Mean to Be Mean?

Hostility and guardedness are born out of a sense of threat to our happiness. The tendency to give in to the suspicion of such a threat results in the development of unintentional hostile behaviors. Let's say you are walking down the street and someone you don't know calls out, "Hey there." Your immediate response will be tainted with a fair degree of suspicion, even when you are not facing any particular threat. The very sense of threat and the ensuing suspicion and guardedness are the general ingredients for hostility.

If our guard were more relaxed, we could be more sympathetic to others and more aware of the environment beyond ourselves. But the more sensitive we are to any sense of threat to our happiness, the more hostile our attitude becomes. When hostility becomes more powerful and untamed, it becomes meanness.

Nobody wakes up thinking, "Today I'm going to be a mean person." But when our self-absorption is constantly looking for threats to self and self's happiness, we unknowingly allow subtle hostility and meanness to come into our reactions. The more threatened we feel, the more we react or contract into self-centeredness, making this self and its agenda even more important, and our attitude more hostile. Is this not what it means to be mean?

Meanness can be defined as not caring for anything above and beyond our own happiness. Furthermore, by contracting into self-centeredness, we become less and less aware of the environment around us. When we think about all the irrational, neurotic behaviors in the world today, we can see how they have become such tremendous displays of hostility and meanness, all for one simple reason: the threat to one's own happiness is seen as the biggest threat. When this perspective is allowed to rule, confusion and neurosis become limitless. Of course, one way or another, all the ensuing anger, desire, ignorance, and other such negativities are quickly justified. But this does not stop the irrational movements we make from a place of meanness, solely in service of our own happiness.

> Whatever pain we afflict on others will inevitably—
> immediately or in the long run—boomerang back.

And the story doesn't end there. From the perspective of the Buddhist teachings, you, by yourself, do not create a singular, individual movement. This unceasing movement—the basic characteristic of all sentient beings—connects all beings. So whatever we say or do, whatever actions we create within this complex play of unceasing movement will impact others. And in turn, their reactions will directly or indirectly influence us back. We can call this the boomerang effect.

It's as if each one of us is trying to score a goal—which we do marvelously well. But our habitual attitudes and tendencies always come with karmic consequences. Whatever pain we afflict on others will inevitably—immediately or in the long run—boomerang back. The first line of the Buddha's teachings, "Do not do anything unvirtuous," refers to not creating, harboring, or cultivating any attitude or action that is hurtful to yourself or others.

No one ever claimed samsara was perfect. In this imperfect world of ours, with everyone propelled by the search for happiness, it is only appropriate that those with awareness, wisdom, and freedom of choice—and most importantly, those equipped with the means of the Dharma—should be the first to abandon what is unvirtuous and cultivate everything that is virtuous. Simply put, since unvirtuous action is born of intolerance, virtuous action is the act of being more tolerant. Keeping in mind the impermanence and interdependence of this seemingly solid self, let go of attitudes that are intolerant and irrational. Let go of self-cherishing behaviors that are guarded, hostile, and mean. When your every thought, word, and deed are driven by the happiness of the self alone, meanness and hostility will never be allowed to fall away.

Simply relaxing our extreme guardedness toward the world relaxes hostility. This in turn creates a little more space within the habitual response of meanness for tolerance to arise. The space for tolerance comes about when our search for happiness is not completely blind to others' same search for happiness.

What Does It Mean to Be Tolerant?

The Tibetan word *zopa* is often translated into English as "patience" or "tolerance." To maintain or familiarize oneself with patience is known as *zogom*. Bear in mind that patience, or tolerance, in this context is not a passive state. This tolerance has various aspects, such as nonviolence, generosity, kindness, and the practice of *bodhichitta*, or selflessness. These qualities are often mistakenly seen as passive states. They may seem to say that you shouldn't defend yourself or stand up for yourself, that you allow yourself to be too vulnerable. But tolerance is anything but a passive state.

To be tolerant is to be courageously patient. It requires awareness, wisdom, and wakefulness in every movement. It requires you to be honest and brave in freeing yourself from overwhelming self-absorption and the enormous influence of the self's search for its own happiness. Then you can do what is right instead of doing only what you like. This is a very proactive state.

Acting out, on the other hand, is always easier: somebody lashes out at you and you lash out back. When your adrenaline is aroused, it is always tempting to take immediate action as an immediate solution. It seems exciting to just get out there, actively solving problems, confronting and expressing them outwardly. But this often just aggravates things and perpetuates the suffering and pain. Ultimately isn't the point to find happiness and bring about an end to suffering and pain? To this end, there is a quote from the Indian philosopher Nagarjuna that I find very inspiring:

> Just as the moon coming out of an eclipse is more gentle
>   and bright,
> we must come out of our past habits even better,
> and with an even brighter illuminating awareness.

Just as the moon slowly and gradually emerges from an eclipse, changing one's habitual reactions takes time and patience. This is particularly true when it comes to changing the habitual response to provocations. When you decide not to react in kind, not to lash out, not to reply in anger—this takes effort and awareness. It is anything but passive! Like the light of the moon emerging from an eclipse brighter and gentler than before, every time habitual reactions are left behind, awareness and tolerance emerge even brighter and more beautiful. Thus, every time we resist the temptation to react habitually, we decrease suffering in the world. When understood correctly, tolerance in the face of adversities actually enables us to find the true happiness we seek.

Now, it is important to remember that the transformation of samsaric qualities into the qualities of a bodhisattva doesn't happen overnight. Just because you feel inspired to act virtuously doesn't mean that tomorrow morning you will suddenly awaken free of all that is unvirtuous. This is a step-by-step process, and these steps are taken within, not outside of you.

It is a process called taming and training the mind—and it is the ground of the bodhisattva path.

BODHISATTVAS ARE VERY COOL

The young people I meet are always talking about being "cool." At some point, I had to ask, "What does it mean to be cool?" From the many explanations I received, I can now say that bodhisattvas are very cool.

I have heard that the definition of cool can be used to describe a state of well-being, a transcendent state, or an internal state of serenity and that cool is an absence of conflict, a state of harmony and intrinsic balance. If these terms are the definition of cool, then perhaps we could say that bodhisattvas are cool. Most importantly, this cool is not about indifference or not caring. But rather, a bodhisattva's cool is about not getting sucked into the whirlpool of emotions that impede the clarity of our own awareness.

For us constantly moving sentient beings, it might be very helpful to cultivate a bodhisattva's cool. We could learn to bring more stillness to our movement and to not be driven by the feelings of threat and fear that are the basis of all unvirtuous actions. By contrast, we could see that the mind of a bodhisattva is open and flexible. By not responding with a sense of threat and fear, we too could become more flexible.

With a more flexible attitude, a bodhisattva's response to events is based upon a greater vision: a vision of what is most needed rather than what is most convenient. Yes, we all want happiness, and no one wants to meet with suffering and pain. But where does that true happiness come from? It comes from having a vision that is greater than the linear perspective of self-absorption. In many Mahayana texts, you can read about the aspirations of bodhisattvas and their expressed desire to be of benefit to sentient beings in whatever way is beneficial. In every situation, a bodhisattva sees what is most needed and helpful and becomes just that. A true bodhisattva can manifest as anything, as wind where wind is needed or sunshine where sunshine is needed. You could think of this metaphorically, as just a way of looking at things. But in actuality, this is the bodhisattva's way of being in the world.

A bodhisattva is not one who simply sits on a throne. In fact, a bodhisattva is a being who has lost any fixed identity. Always remember that. What does it mean to truly practice the teachings on helping others? It means letting go of your own identity and concentrating on whatever is needed at the moment. You could be a father or a mother, a teacher or a student, if and when you must. It would be just another fixation to think that as a man, you couldn't be helpful in a feminine way; that as a teacher, you couldn't be a practitioner; or as a practitioner, you couldn't be a teacher. Such fixations are what a Buddhist practitioner is trying to be free of. This is perhaps what being a Buddhist is really about.

This is also what the basic discipline of sitting meditation, especially shamatha meditation, is about. The Sanskrit word *shamatha*, or *zhine* in Tibetan, means "peaceful abiding." In sitting meditation, we work with the stickiness of mind's habitual neurotic patterns: those causes of suffering and obscurations of our inherent nature of goodness and happiness. Working with the body, mind, and breath in sitting meditation allows us to cut through the stickiness of habitual fixations.

CONTEMPLATION

In meditation, begin with the willingness to turn away from habitual patterns of confusion, distractions, and speediness. Train in letting the mind rest free from hope and fear—and do not try to generate any concepts or spiritual "events." Just rest. Simply allow your mind to be open and spacious. For those of you just setting out on the path of meditation, it is always helpful to begin with personal and proper instruction. For those already familiar with meditation, always support your path with diligence and discipline.

AWAKE TO RIGHT CHOICES

If like all sentient beings, or *drowa semchen*, you and I are in constant movement, what sets us human beings apart from all other kinds of beings? It is the fact that we are endowed with intelligence and wonderful capabilities. These arise as the fruit of merit and virtue, and they endow our human lives with wonderful possibilities and choices. Whether or not you realize the qualities and choices you enjoy is entirely up to you. It is your choice whether you live a life of intolerance or a life of tolerance.

If you do realize the potential within you, I encourage you to make the right choices. If calling yourself a Buddhist inspires you to cultivate your inherent basic goodness, then you are a Buddhist. What is most important is to realize the gifts of this human life and then to develop the wisdom and courage to abandon what is unvirtuous and to cultivate what is virtuous.

Virtuous actions can be characterized by awareness and the ability to go beyond self-cherishing, intolerant behavior. For this, my advice is to always keep things simple. The many Mahayana and Vajrayana forms of teachings, methods, and instructions on training the mind exist simply to bring about this recognition. If one gets this simple message, it really is not necessary to become busy with all these many methods. The methods are not the destination; they are the means to help us on the path to our destination.

As simple as this is, though, it requires courage to go beyond grasping on to our own happiness and to consider the happiness of others. The impulse to protect our own happiness and space propels us into the comfortable habit of intolerance. And at such times, we may think it is very difficult to change intolerance into tolerance or grasping into non-grasping. But this is not necessarily true. We are actually very bad at grasping. For example, within the last twenty-four-hour cycle, how many thoughts have you had, and how many of those thoughts do you remember now? Countless thoughts have passed through your mind, but when you try to recall them, you may find that, other than having a vague recollection, you don't remember those thoughts at all.

Unless we fixate very strongly on a thought, most conceptual thoughts pass through the mind without our grasping on to them and without amounting to much of anything at all. Compared to the number of thoughts we may remember or fixate upon, there are many more thoughts that we do not remember or hold onto. So we can see, we are actually much better at not grasping than grasping. This natural talent for not grasping is what you have to tap into. As you grow older, you may say that your memory isn't what it was, but you should take great delight and joy in that! Now you are blessed with the ability to not grasp. It is often a blessing when things leave you instead of you trying to let them go. And in any case, what do you do with what you remember? Nothing extraordinary. The few things we grasp on to usually become problematic because of the distortions, exaggerations, or importance we bring to them. So, why not declutter and clean up?

In order to harness the qualities and opportunities of this precious human life, we must make right choices. We must choose to cultivate tolerance, selflessness, and virtue. To cultivate tolerance, we must resist the habitual tendency to contract into self-absorption, selfishness, and meanness. This is easy because we are naturally, by nature, tolerant. To cultivate selflessness, we can choose to emulate the bodhisattvas by letting go of grasping and by manifesting in whatever ways and forms are most needed by others. If we act in these ways, with awareness and kindness, virtue is the result. It is that simple.

Mistaken Tolerance

We may think that only bodhisattvas are naturally tolerant, or patient, but tolerance is a natural capacity that we all possess. Recognizing our own capacity for tolerance is the first step. All too often, however, that tolerance is mistaken.

What is mistaken tolerance? Consider this example: Many of us live in places where there are very high levels of noise pollution. With noise coming from machines, music, traffic, people, animals, and horns, we become desensitized over time to this constant noise. We no longer notice it. We become habituated to the noise around us. Likewise, many of us seem to shrug at our various inner pollutants: afflicted emotions such as anger, jealousy, ego, and self-absorption. We've become accustomed to them, and we don't question when they arise. But this tolerance for habitual reactions is mistaken. Why would we have such tolerance for our own afflicted emotions—and so little patience for those of others?

Tolerance is mistaken when the need arises for immediate gratification in our search for happiness. Our impatience is experienced as restlessness, which fuels the inclination toward movement. Movement—the fundamental characteristic of a sentient being—is strongly linked to impatience. This restlessness, therefore, has to be calmed down. Then, the energy of our natural tolerance can be given the right guidance. In this way, the energy of intolerance can be transformed.

When restlessness is combined with intolerance, sometimes we get immediate results. Here is a traditional example: You are placed in a dark room with a bow, some arrows, and a target to hit. Because you're shooting in the dark, you miss most of the time. But occasionally you may strike the target—which makes you think you are happy. You forget the misses. You think, "I can do this. I can shoot in the dark and still hit the target." The target here, in the context of intolerance, is your own happiness. Driven by impatience, you may find that anger does get you some satisfaction, being jealous does get you a win, and thinking only of yourself does serve you well. You're shooting in the dark, but you concentrate on the hits and not the misses. Therefore, you justify intolerance and impatience, which then makes it easier to act out. It may even bring some happiness or sense of accomplishment. "Yes," you might conclude, "anger does help me to defend myself. It protects my self-respect, my safety, my space." The sense that "this works" sticks in your psyche—the sense that, even shooting in the dark, you got a hit. This then becomes a strong basis for sustaining habitual patterns.

When negativity becomes a habit, we begin to increasingly identify with our intolerance and impatience. It seems reasonable to act neurotically. But like any addiction, what seems to be a cause for happiness in the beginning eventually becomes a trap. Then we start getting more misses than hits. That's the reality. Sustained by the nostalgia of having had a hit, we allow ourselves to be very tolerant of our neuroses—but neuroses are no source of happiness. What then would the transformation of this intolerance look like?

If there were Buddhist before-and-after pictures, we could call them "primordial" and "now." Our primordial pictures—not in the once-upon-a-time sense but rather in the sense of our original state—would give a sense of who we are by nature rather than how we appear to be now. They would show our tremendous capacity for contentment, not our constant dissatisfaction. They would show our immense capacity to be joyful and loving and not our anxiety and stress. And they would show our fundamentally good nature with all its wonderful qualities and not the "after" of mistaken tolerance. By recognizing the energy of tolerance "gone wrong," we can move that energy in the right direction. In this way, as the Mahayana teachings point out, we are able to generate empathy for others by understanding the nature of our own intolerance.

CONTEMPLATION

In the beginning, it can be challenging to be tolerant, or patient. But if you truly wish for happiness, you will find that directing your natural tolerance in the right direction is a truer source of happiness than impatience and negativity. Begin by recognizing how the care and feeding of impatience fuels the habitual patterns of anger, jealousy, and desire. By transforming impatience into tolerance, you will then see the need for a deep, sympathetic understanding of others.

SYMPATHETIC UNDERSTANDING BORN OF EGO

When joined with awareness and discernment, this self-cherishing ego can become the reference for cherishing others.

The Buddha taught that the ego mind that cherishes the self is the same mind that gives birth to the enlightened, or *bodhi*, mind. With awareness and discernment, this self-cherishing ego can become our reference for cherishing others. This is called sympathetic understanding. By first recognizing our own restless energy and intolerance, we can see how strong such habits can be. And we can develop a more sympathetic understanding of others who react in the same way.

This sympathetic attitude requires careful introspection, discrimination, and awareness. By observing our own actions and reactions, we can see the restless, impatient energy that aspires to our own happiness alone. Seeing our own self-cherishing allows us to know how others feel. Reflecting on our own tendency to give in to misguided tolerance becomes our reference for being tolerant of others. In this way, our own intolerant, self-cherishing energy can change into a deep awareness that every other sentient being in movement, every *drowa*, feels the same way. From sympathetic understanding, a more genuine compassion is born.

In the Mahayana teachings, compassion is the key to transforming intolerance into genuine tolerance. This is a step-by-step process of direct experience and introspection. Without such introspection, compassion is just an emotion or an acquired knowledge. Acquired knowledge is shallow and easy to forget. A word like *bodhichitta*, for example, can be quickly read or conceptually understood, without us really experiencing it or knowing what it means. Without introspection and direct experience, the teachings could become dogmatic and not necessarily to the point.

After months of traveling and teaching around the world, I remember very often returning home and complaining to my teacher about various issues related to students and practitioners. During the course of one such discussion, he stopped me abruptly with a simple question: "Do you really like the people you work with?" This stopped me and made me think carefully. To my surprise, I found that while I did not necessarily dislike them, I didn't particularly like them either. This exchange has been an extremely important teaching for me. It clearly pointed out the importance of realizing that—before I could have any hope of ever demonstrating compassion for all sentient beings—I had to take the first small step. I had to cultivate the sympathetic attitude that sees the sameness of all sentient beings' experiences. Once I was able to appreciate the sameness of our experiences, I could take the next step toward genuine empathy or compassion for others.

To develop a sympathetic attitude that will eventually blossom into compassion, you start by first training the mind to see and listen to others. Then you will have a deeper understanding of their hopes and fears, which are no different from your own. You have to be brave enough to look straight into the eyes of their pain and suffering and see their hunger and anxiety and insecurities beneath the makeup and polite words. And then you will see clearly how the habit of self-cherishing leads to the many ways we all react and act out.

Our modern societies have become very adept at covering up and packaging things very beautifully. No matter what the actual content of the package may be, most of the effort seems to go into the packaging. We work hard to hide and conceal anything that looks ugly, sad, or inefficient. This emphasis on outer appearance over inner content can easily influence our minds. When we look at each other, for example, if the outer appearances look fine, we may fail to see any inner struggles. We are misled to think that since everything is fine on the outside, everything is fine on the inside. We won't take the time to appreciate whatever inner struggles someone might be experiencing. Our reliance on outer appearances makes it difficult to develop a sympathetic attitude, and it keeps us from any true understanding of suffering.

Today, many people try to understand the concept of suffering through books. Of course, some of you will say that you certainly do understand what suffering is: you are suffering a disease, a divorce, or the loss of your job, your money, or your home. That is indeed suffering. But it doesn't necessarily mean that your mind has opened up to the manifold and diverse experiences of suffering, which other sentient beings in this world are going through.

We tend to forget the fact that the true nature of samsara is suffering and to rely instead on beautiful packaging. Such a mistaken perspective causes us to become more absorbed in the bubbles of our own experiences—which, in turn, fuels our intolerance toward others. Then rather than opening the mind up with a deep sympathetic understanding of others, we may just keep chasing one beautiful bubble after another. And in the chase, we may forget how to live with one another.

Four Simple Steps

There is a beautiful example of how to cultivate sympathetic understanding in four simple steps:

First, let sympathetic understanding knock.
Second, open the door and let it enter.

Third, welcome it and allow it to rest.

Fourth, aspire to hold sympathy for others within your heart.

When someone wishes to enter a house, they first knock on the door (step 1). Hearing the knock, you open the door and welcome the person in (step 2). In the same way, when the sympathetic attitude knocks at the door of your heart, open the door of your heart and let it in. Welcome it and allow it to rest there (step 3). This becomes your aspiration to hold sympathy for others within your heart (step 4).

In practice, when any thought or experience of empathy knocks at the door of your heart, it is important that you open the door and let it fully enter your mindstream. Welcome this sympathetic understanding. Make sure to open the doors of your heart and mind wide enough to truly understand what another sentient being is going through. If you are unable to do this, you will find yourself living in a bubble of selfishness, shut off in a world with only three inhabitants: me, myself, and I. In this case, no matter how much you meditate or whatever else you do, compassion will remain only an idea, without the necessary power to transform your attitude.

True compassion means allowing introspection and understanding to knock on the door of your heart. Allow it to enter. Welcome it as you would welcome a guest. Allow this awareness to rest and feel comfortable in the space of your heart and mind. When it becomes more constant in your mindstream, use it as the basis of a deeper understanding of others' wish for happiness and freedom from their manifold states of suffering. In this way, the transition from self-cherishing to the cherishing of others becomes more natural, and everything that occurs within the vastness of mind can be handled with the grace and elegance of kindness.

Accomplishing these four steps is called accomplishing "aspiration bodhichitta": the wish for the happiness of all sentient beings. Whenever you feel a strong wish to find happiness and to be free from suffering, whenever you are going through various experiences of hope and fear, happiness and suffering, use these moments to deepen your awareness of others. Through your own experience, you can learn to recognize that this is exactly how all other sentient beings experience the same thing. This is the basis of sympathetic understanding. When your own ego-cherishing becomes the reference for cherishing others, that is the beginning of bodhi mind: a bodhisattva's mind.

We do not begin the journey on the bodhisattva path without ego. The self-cherishing ego is there, but its movements can be moved in the right direction. That same ego can become your reference for learning about the ego-cherishing of all sentient beings. When ego's natural propensity for movement moves in the right direction, we learn what it means to move away from the cause of suffering and toward true happiness for ourselves and others. In short, moving your mind in the right direction liberates the mind from the causes of suffering. This is what is meant by "training the mind."

CONTEMPLATION

Just as a perfectly clean and beautiful lotus grows from a muddy pond, let the experience of your own self-cherishing ego be your reference for understanding others. From your own struggles with ego, allow yourself to recognize that all sentient beings struggle in the same way in their pursuit of happiness and freedom from suffering. Let your own intolerance for threats to your happiness be a reference for understanding others' intolerance. Let the importance of your own hopes and fears allow you to understand the play of others' hopes and fears—and the pain of not moving the mind in the right direction.

FOUR

Training the Mind

We have to grab the bull by the horns, so to speak. For that,
we need to examine what we mean by "mind."

TAMING AND TRAINING the mind require us to direct the mind
away from the causes that bring about suffering. This takes some
work. Our lack of awareness and lack of sympathetic introspection
have become habits. To break us free from these habits, it is helpful to practice and study the Dharma, to receive teachings and to
meditate. But in the Buddhist teachings—and in our own search for
happiness and freedom from suffering—what is essential is training
the mind.

Mind is the basis of all experiences. It is the mind that experiences happiness and suffering. Our happiness is not independent
of mind; our unwanted suffering and pain are not independent of
mind. They originate in the mind and are dependent on mind. The
happiness and suffering that propel all of our movements are both
products of mind. It stands to reason that we would want to understand mind and not just mind's products. Therefore, it is essential to
emphasize the third line uttered by Shariputra to Mahakashyapa as
he summarized the Buddha's teachings: "Train the mind."

To tame and train the mind, we cannot just imagine some abstract mind and think, "I'm going to train that." We have to grab the bull by the horns, so to speak. For that, we need to examine what we mean by "mind." The subject of mind has intrigued many throughout time. But mind has always remained abstract—something somewhere between the brain and the heart. Within the Buddhist teachings, the subject of mind—how it functions and what its nature is—is a pivotal subject.

MIND'S EIGHT LEVELS OF CONSCIOUSNESS

Mind and its nature are taught extensively within the different schools of Buddhism and are therefore approached in various ways. From the Mahayana perspective, this mind is not necessarily one singular mind; *mind* is a generic term for eight levels of consciousness. There are the five sense consciousnesses of the ears, eyes, nose, tongue, and touch. There is the sixth consciousness, known as the mind, or mental, consciousness. The seventh consciousness is called the afflictive consciousness, and the eighth consciousness is known as the *alaya*, or ground, consciousness.

The five sense consciousnesses have the ability to experience specific things. Their limitation is that they can only experience these things. The eye consciousness can see. The ear consciousness can hear. The nose consciousness can smell and breathe. The tongue consciousness can taste. And the physical body's tactile consciousness can feel temperature and textural sensations.

The sixth sense consciousness, known as the mental consciousness, is able to discriminate among all those sensory experiences. The limitation of the sixth consciousness is that it can only discern one experience in any given moment. For example, when you look out your window and see a tree, your eye consciousness is active. Then you hear a bird call out, and your ear consciousness is now active. And then you feel the breeze on your skin, and the body's tactile consciousness is active. The moment your ear consciousness is engaged, you have moved away from your eye consciousness. The moment that your tactile sensations are engaged, you have moved away from your ear consciousness, and so on. This is an important observation. The sixth consciousness, the mental consciousness, simply discerns, or notices, the movement between one consciousness and another.

The seventh consciousness, the afflictive consciousness, imputes a sense of "I," or identity, onto the activity of the sense perceptions. It is called afflicted because it is from this sense of "I," or ego, that all afflictions are born. The eighth consciousness, the ground consciousness, is seen as the basis from which all the other consciousnesses arise. In the context of taming the mind and abandoning what is unvirtuous and cultivating virtue, it is important to learn how the eighth consciousness functions.

In short, while our five sense consciousnesses remain busy with the movement of various sensory experiences, with each sensory experience—thanks to the sixth sense consciousness—habitual discrimination comes up. Therefore, this sixth consciousness and its discrimination of sensory experience need to be thoroughly examined first.

THE SIXTH SENSE: MENTAL CONSCIOUSNESS

The ability to discriminate what you like, dislike, or feel neutral about originates from the sixth, or mental, consciousness. Having identified good and bad, you want more of the good and none of the bad. The third option is a neutral or gray area: you are not clear about wanting or not wanting even though there is still some recognition or discrimination of an experience. Some people mistakenly think this neutral discrimination is a good thing or see it as nondiscriminatory. But this isn't the case. A neutral attitude is not an absence of confusion; it is often actually more confused or simply so lazy it can't even decide.

Just as the other five consciousnesses have limitations, the mental consciousness also has a limitation. While it does have the ability to differentiate sensory experiences, its limitation is that it can only differentiate one at a time. So, while the five outward-looking senses are busily engaged in a variety of sensory experiences through the five sense doors, the mental consciousness must try to keep up. With the continuous flow and speed of sensory experiences, however, the sixth consciousness becomes limited in its ability to discern clearly.

It may seem that we can see, think, eat, speak, taste, and smell simultaneously. Multitasking may seem to make sense. But when we examine this discriminating mental consciousness carefully, we find that when it thinks, it can only respond to thinking, and when it sees something, it can only respond to what it sees. When it hears something, it has to drop what it is seeing in order to respond to what is being heard.

This busy, rapid, and constant movement of the sense consciousnesses, and the mental consciousness's discrimination of those experiences is the movement we have been talking about all along. To work with your own mind, it is very important to understand these two movements: the experiences brought about by the five sense consciousnesses and the discrimination of experience brought about by the sixth, or mental, consciousness.

The Ignorance of Monkey Mind

A traditional Buddhist analogy for the outward movement of the sense consciousnesses is a house with five windows and a monkey inside. The monkey has nothing to do inside the empty house, so it pops its head out of the various windows, full of curiosity and in search of sensory experiences. This energy of curiosity, busily experiencing and discriminating, is called "monkey mind."

There are, in fact, three energies going on at the moment of perception. Along with experiencing and discriminating, there is something called "self-awareness," or *rangrig* in Tibetan. This is a subtle inner awareness of our experiencing and discriminating, our liking and disliking. But because the energies of experiencing and discriminating are so strong, this subtle self-awareness is usually overridden. This is what is meant by the "ignorance" of a distracted or untamed mind. Although that pervasive subtle awareness is our nature, it is suppressed by the monkey mind, which is so involved in its outer sensory experiences and its habit of unnecessary discrimination. Overworked by the movement of constant discrimination, the monkey mind loses clarity and clear discernment. In this way, our subtle awareness becomes veiled by the ignorance of outer movement. This always reminds me of my Buddhist friends who like to gather outside on beautiful days for lunch in between teaching sessions. They eat, they gossip, they savor the food and wine, and enjoy the sunshine—all the while trying to be intelligent Buddhists carrying on profound discussions.

Now to fully engage with each of these many sensory experiences, the discriminating mental consciousness must keep up. When you pick up your fork, you must know exactly how to aim it toward your mouth. While your tongue is busy with the taste of food, you might also be talking about emptiness or some other profound topic. And you are not only aware of the topic, you are also aware of the person you are speaking with—and whether or not you agree with them. All of these sensations and emotions seem to be happening simultaneously.

If the mental consciousness, which can only discriminate one experience at a time, becomes overloaded, imagine how overloaded our subtle awareness becomes at that point. It is not that our awareness is absent. Awareness is basically always there; it has been there all along. But awareness is dominated by unceasing outer experiences and by the busyness of the mental consciousness trying to discriminate every experience in its rapid-fire way. If the mental consciousness can only differentiate one experience at a time, how much hope is there for awareness at that moment? In this way, our subtle awareness becomes clouded.

Meditation as Antidote to Constant Movement

Until we can calm the busyness of sensory experiences and mental discrimination, we cannot tame the mind. This is what we are doing when we meditate to train the mind. And this is why, when we talk about training the mind in Buddhism, so much emphasis is placed on settling the senses into stillness.

It is Buddhist meditation that emphasizes the three crucial points of stillness, silence, and non-thought. For a beginner, meditation provides the framework for settling the busy movement of the five senses. This then allows the discriminating mental consciousness to also settle. With the slowing down of the sixth consciousness's tendency to engage with all sensory experiences, there is more space for clearer discernment and clarity.

In this way, meditation becomes one of the most powerful antidotes to our habit of constant movement. The settledness that comes with the slowing down of the momentum of the five sense consciousnesses provides clarity to the mental consciousness. When not overloaded with sensory discrimination, the mental consciousness can actually develop deeper introspection.

This introspection is both outward and inward. Outwardly, there is the constant outer movement and discrimination of sense perceptions. But, inwardly, who is it that actually has all of these preferences, these likes and dislikes? This kind of introspection gives pause to all the outer movement obscuring our inner subtle awareness. Instead, there is a sense of someone who actually sees you experiencing the five sense consciousnesses, someone who sees you liking and disliking them. At this point, we are calling that someone "awareness." Not manipulating our awareness is called meditation.

The Drama of Total Immersion

Training the mind simply means reducing the total immersion and manipulation of your awareness.

According to the Mahayana teachings, there are two aspects of awareness: outward awareness, or *zhenrig* in Tibetan, and inner self-awareness, or *rangrig*. In order to train the mind, both aspects of awareness need to be understood. When awareness is totally immersed in sensory experiences and discrimination about those experiences, this is called outward awareness. There is awareness, but it is outwardly immersed, like being totally immersed in a movie.

When some of us watch a movie, for example, we drown ourselves in it fully. If you've ever watched a horror film, you might remember becoming terrified by scenes that you could only bear to watch through half-covered eyes. And then there are the very dramatic movies, the tearjerkers: the father dies, a mother dies, a child is lost, or great global disasters happen. But if someone were to ask, "Why would you willingly allow yourself to become so immersed and so sad about a drama on the screen?" you would probably answer, "I enjoy it!"

These are good examples of total immersion into whatever is being "projected." In the case of a movie, of course, we all know what to expect. We come with boxes of tissues or rolls of toilet paper, ready to weep. Likewise, we experience total immersion in similar types of projections and life experiences. In Buddhist terminology, this kind of immersion into whatever is being projected is referred to as "distraction." But although we call it distraction, we are not without awareness. There is awareness, even if that awareness is totally immersed and manipulated by our outward focus. Training the mind simply means reducing the total immersion and manipulation of our awareness. How is this done? It is done by letting the sense experiences and our immersion in them simply be.

There are various ways to train in "letting be," such as shamatha and vipashyana meditation, and the various postures, gazes, and ways of working with the breath. By training in these various methods, a meditator can begin to calm down the physical sense consciousnesses by bringing them into single-pointed focus, such as the breath. Other meditation methods train one to direct the energies of the sixth consciousness, the discriminating mental consciousness, in the right direction. Most importantly, we always have to begin by taking the first step.

The first step in training this monkey mind is always to train the monkey to sit quietly. You teach the monkey to sit quietly by closing the windows of the sense consciousnesses for short periods of time. This is done by simply allowing the sense consciousnesses to rest. Instead of focusing on each and every sensory experience, simply let them be.

Next, you tell the monkey that it is okay not to constantly discriminate. This one is more difficult because you are habituated to thinking that all sensory experiences need your discrimination. You tell yourself that everyone expects you to have an opinion or a judgment; you expect yourself to have opinions and judgments, which you have come to believe are important. The habit of discriminating is aggravated even more by the assumption that you are clever; the assumption that you know it all fuels this habit.

In today's culture especially, not having an opinion is often equated with being stupid. Therefore, breaking free from this habit becomes all the more difficult. By training the mind in meditation, the habit of constantly having opinions and passing judgments on every sensory experience is given a rest. Thinking that the whole world depends on your discriminating mind is given a rest.

CONTEMPLATION

If you really wish to train your mind, find random moments throughout the day in which to calm down the busyness of sensory experiences and the habit of discrimination. In these small pockets of time, stop being so distracted by experiences and give pause to the tendency to bring discrimination to what you do experience.

Even better, relax with these experiences and let the discriminations be! You might think you don't know how to do this, but that is not true. The next time you go to bed, just before you sink into sleep, notice how experiences settle. As you relax further, notice too that you stop discriminating, that you are naturally able to just let things be. At that moment, your mind is free of any grasping to experiences. You could remain in this moment of awareness, free and unencumbered by sense experiences and mental discrimination. Of course, instead of remaining aware in this moment, it is more likely that you will fall asleep.

THE EIGHTH CONSCIOUSNESS

Before discussing the seventh consciousness, let's look briefly at the eighth consciousness. When you begin to fall asleep, you stop indulging in sense experiences and discrimination. All of the six consciousnesses—the five sense consciousnesses and the sixth, mental, consciousness—withdraw and merge into an indefinable blank state. This is usually called "dissolving into the eighth consciousness," which is the base, or ground, consciousness known in Sanskrit as the *alaya*.

Although there is a semblance of non-grasping and settledness while in this state, there is also an absence of awareness. It is more of an absorbed, blank state and not a state of pure ground consciousness. Nevertheless, it is a helpful reference for seeing how awareness dissolves back into the ground consciousness. This, you realize, is something that you do all the time.

Between the moment when all six consciousnesses dissolve and the moment you fully fall asleep, you could tap into the energy of the ground consciousness. In most ordinary circumstances, this moment is so brief that we fail to recognize it. However, for beginners on the path of trying to understand how mind functions, it is helpful to try. Just before falling asleep, try to observe the presence of the ground consciousness in this common, everyday experience, when the six senses dissolve and one is aware of but not indulging in sensory experiences.

The importance of understanding the eight consciousnesses forms a very important part of the Mahayana. Teachings on Madhyamaka, Mahamudra, and Dzogchen further elaborate on its nature. From the point of view of taming the mind, Mahayana and Vajrayana teachings both emphasize examining and understanding the movement of the eight consciousnesses, and many forms of meditation are prescribed to train meditators in going beyond the movements of the first seven consciousnesses and settling into the ground consciousness.

WHAT ABOUT THE SEVENTH CONSCIOUSNESS?

The reason we have not spoken much about the seventh consciousness so far is because it doesn't really exist—at least not in the way we may think it does. In the Mahayana teachings, the seventh consciousness is called the "afflictive consciousness," or *nyon yi* in Tibetan. Simply put, it is the sense of an "I," or self. Instead of seeing this subtle expression of energy as our innate awareness, we mistakenly give it an identity. This imposition of an "I" is what we come to believe is directing our experiences and constant discrimination of the six sense consciousnesses.

We end up not only giving this energy an identity but also gradually allowing it to create a stronghold over all of our experiences. This stronghold is called "ego-grasping." Upon careful examination, we will clearly see the nonexistence of this ego, or self. Nevertheless, the energy of the sense of self and its suppositions is quite neurotic, or afflicted. And the more importance we give to this "I"-that-doesn't-actually-exist, the further we separate from our own true nature. This is why the Buddhist teachings emphasize careful examination of topics such as the nature of self, letting go of self-attachment, and the emptiness nature of self. According to these teachings, our ground nature is naturally pure and clear. However, when we grasp on to that clarity—and even worse, when that grasping leads to the assumption of a subjective self—this is the basis of the affliction. When the seventh, or afflictive, consciousness is left unchallenged and sustained over time, it becomes the source of all delusions.

The Power of Mind

To tame this mind, we must first train in settling into the pervasive state of our awareness. It is within this settled awareness, left free from discrimination and ego-grasping, that we are able to see clearly the power of mind.

Why do you need to tame your mind? Why is this your responsibility? Such questions can be answered more clearly when you see and appreciate how powerful your mind is and, since it is your mind, how the responsibility for it is also yours. All experiences of happiness and suffering are the products of this mind. What would be the reality of any experience, beyond your own mind experiencing it? As is said in one of the greatest teachings of the Buddha, the *Lankavatara Sutra*:

> Whatever *is* is mind.
> Mind is the artist.

That is, since mind is the artist, whatever *is* is drawn by the mind. It is your mind that designs happiness and suffering. Examining mind in this way, we see its basic nature, its various expressions, and how our assumptions create flawed ideas about mind. Seeing that this powerful mind is the artist that creates all of our experiences, we can also appreciate the responsibility we have to train this mind. Since everything stems from our own mind, we work to tame the mind in such a way that this powerful mind abandons everything unvirtuous and cultivates what is virtuous.

This is what was taught by the Buddha—but this teaching is beyond any religious discourse. It simply illuminates the basic responsibility of being human: that we are human beings with beautiful, powerful minds. This is what the Buddha discovered.

Meditation and Mind

By carefully observing and learning how mind functions, train your mind.

From one point of view, the whole spectrum of mind training, or what we call meditation, can be best understood within the context of the eight consciousnesses.

This progressive stage of taming the mind requires one to first tame the five physical sense consciousnesses to be less overwhelmed by the sights, sounds, smells, tastes, and tactile sensations they experience.

Instead, mind is trained to settle into a state of letting be. To quiet the mind in this way, you begin by quieting the body and quieting speech. To settle the body, you take the right meditation posture. To settle speech, you are silent. Settling the body into the meditation posture and settling speech into silence prepares the ground for working with the subtler sixth consciousness, the mental consciousness.

This can be done by way of most forms of *shamatha* meditation. The word *shamatha*, or *zhine* in Tibetan, means "peaceful abiding." Shamatha meditation emphasizes a settled awareness, wherein one is not seduced by the activities of the five sense consciousnesses. It also gives rest to the habitual impulse to discriminate experiences. In this way, one trains to cultivate a pervasive, undistracted resting that is gently awake but free of any discriminating or grasping to whatever arises in the field of one's awareness.

Once the meditator is able to stabilize this settled awareness, they train further in *vipashyana* meditation. The word *vipashyana*, or *lhagtong* in Tibetan, means "clear seeing." One not only abides in an undistracted state but also learns to investigate and question the reality and true nature of that supposed "I," the seventh consciousness. This all goes back to the third line of Shariputra's verse: "Train the mind." And this brings us to the path of Dharma.

CONTEMPLATION

In order to begin to tame the mind, learn to settle the habitual impulse to grasp on to experiences and to unnecessarily burden them with discrimination. Then investigate the reality of the "something" that seems to dictate these impulsive habits: something that goes by the name "ego." By carefully observing and learning how the mind functions, train your mind.

In order to generate happiness and the causes of happiness, and to find freedom from suffering and the causes of suffering, it is imperative to tame and train the mind.

PART TWO

Getting to the Heart
of Practice

FIVE

On the Path of Dharma

Walking the path of Dharma is important because we cannot underestimate the power of habit.

THE EXAMPLES OF IGNORANCE, greed, and aggression that we are witnessing around the world today evoke the Buddha's teachings in an almost allegorical way. The Buddha characterized ignorance as the reluctance to look inward and examine clearly. Today, our consciousnesses are increasingly driven outward through the pathways of the senses. There they become stupefied by marvelous illusions, which in turn give rise to attachment and aggression. As we pursue these external attractions—forms, sounds, concepts, and so on—we become more and more entangled in their play.

When we begin to get a hint of the elusiveness of that play—and how it may never ultimately satisfy us—we experience a sense of struggle and ever-increasing discontentment. Feelings of struggle and discontent drive us to pursue external objects even more in the hope of getting what we want or avoiding what we don't want. If we are occasionally lucky enough to get what we want, this spurs us on more—even when, for all of our efforts, we ultimately may not really like what we get.

Once, while driving across the United States, we pulled into a truck stop that had one of those mechanical claw machines where you put in a quarter and get a toy. The very first time I put in a quarter, I pulled out a fuzzy toy, which made someone exclaim, "Wow! Of course, Khandro Rinpoche got it!" And I remember clearly how such an experience makes you want to do it again and again. The thrill of getting a fuzzy toy, something that no one really needs or wants, propels you to try again and again. Samsara seems to work in the same way. The attractiveness and elusiveness of sensory experiences, coupled with our successes and failures in pursuit of them, entangle us in the play of samsara—and leave us with no "quarters."

The play of the senses is elusive in that they arise but quickly change and pass away. Their elusiveness challenges us and drives us to engage further in outward activities. But no matter how much we pursue or modify things outside of ourselves, at some point it is just endless activity. In our social lives, in politics, in the environment, in the world at large—the experience of unsettledness and feelings of being unsatiated and discontent often leaves us exhausted. Yet we are driven to continue in this confusion and chaos.

Walking the path of Dharma is important because we cannot underestimate the power of habit. The teachings of the Buddhadharma are very helpful for all of us in this regard. They help us to understand that instead of being driven by illusory, temporary passions and the challenges of incompleteness, we could walk the path of the teachings that help us find rest and contentment within.

IF YOU WANT TO CROSS A RIVER

In one of his first encounters with the Buddha, the sage Mahakashyapa is said to have asked, "What is it that you teach? What is it that we call Dharma? And what is the practice of Dharma, especially in the context of so many forms of worship?"

Mahakashyapa was a Brahman and had sat many long hours in all forms of practice. He was devoted to prayer, meditation, and rituals. Being familiar with all these forms of practice, he asked the Buddha, "Is this Dharma as well? How important are all these things?" To Mahakashyapa's question, the Buddha replied, "They each have their place, and they are all skillful means, but one must never mistake them for being the ultimate Dharma."

This is something to be very clear about. The Buddha was not saying that such things are not important. He was pointing to the subtle difference between the ultimate meaning of Dharma and the many means that support its realization. All too often, we become entangled in these many forms, assuming them to be the ultimate. Engrossed in various practices, we often lose sight of the true meaning of Dharma. We become preoccupied with our appearance as practitioners—with our languages, traditions, recitations, forms, and methods of meditation—rather than allowing these forms to reveal the meaning of Dharma.

Responding to Mahakashyapa, the Buddha asked, "Imagine, Kashyapa, that there is a wide river in front of you and you need to get across it. How would you do it?" Mahakashyapa replied, "If the river is shallow, you could walk across to the other side. Otherwise, you could take a boat, or maybe you could swim to the other shore." The Buddha asked, "But what if you don't want to walk across, you don't know how to swim, and you refuse to take a boat? What if instead, you demanded that the other side of the shore come to you?" Mahakashyapa replied, "Well, that would be a very foolish or stupid person. How could anyone demand such an unreasonable thing?" "Exactly!" said the Buddha.

This beautiful example is very significant in the sutra teachings and one that we need to keep in mind. Some of us who call ourselves Buddhists may be doing our practices with a sense of expectation that the "other shore" come to us. To practice the path of Dharma correctly, you must take everything in your life—all emotions, experiences, and stumbling blocks—into the practice of meditation. This means working with your own mind. Nothing else. The determination to do so is, itself, meditation.

Enlightenment or any realization does not happen because we will it or demand it. Nor does it happen because we belong to a profound lineage, or sit on throne, or intellectualize philosophy. The root of Dharma lies in taming one's mind. The path of Dharma entails using the many methods that support the taming of this mind, and the diligence and patience to do so.

WE NEED A TEACHER

Do you really need a teacher on this path? It is said that our basic nature is the primordially enlightened buddha nature. So it would seem there is no need to rely on any external support. One should be able to simply realize this inherent nature and abide within it unwaveringly.

Unfortunately, however, it is also clear that most of us will encounter many challenges in the form of habitual tendencies, which keep us from accessing and realizing this basic enlightened nature. The causes, conditions, and circumstances of our lives—along with our accumulated habits, attitudes, and stubbornness—are such that we could benefit greatly by relying on a teacher. Therefore, while enlightenment is basically up to us, it is still always helpful to have the support of a spiritual friend. But this is a topic that requires careful reflection and understanding.

The topic of a spiritual friend often raises the subject of the teacher-student relationship: a vast subject that requires careful understanding of what we mean by relationship. I am not sure the word *relationship* is even accurate—or, when it comes to a guru and disciple, whether there even is such a thing. So, what does this word really mean in the Buddhist context? The dictionary says that a *relationship* is the way in which two or more people are connected. But to see the teacher-student relationship in a mundane way, as a "connection" leading to the build-up of further concepts, would be a misunderstanding of what it means to relate to a teacher.

While on the path of Dharma, relating to a teacher, or guru, entails a relationship that has the power to cut through concepts. Through this relationship, the teacher must be able to cut through a student's dualistic concepts, and the student must find the strength and courage to do the same. If, instead, this relationship leads to the building up of further concepts, the relationship becomes complicated. In many situations, it can become destructive, which we see all too often in the spiritual world. Nevertheless, reliance upon a teacher who embodies the necessary pure qualities will provide clarity and support to a student on the path, who is then able to learn and progress in the meaning of Dharma.

What the Word *Guru* Does Not Mean

In general, these days we seem to use the word *teacher* when speaking about our gurus. Many ask me whether this word is appropriate. If the English word *teacher* means someone whose wisdom and compassion is unsurpassable, someone who can cut through your every doubt and hesitation and help you discover within yourself a potential that you never imagined you had, then the word *teacher* may be appropriate. What the word *guru*, or *lama*, does not mean is someone who simply teaches or preaches a doctrine.

The essential meaning of *guru* is vast and profound. A word or sentence would fail to capture its full meaning. Today, however, the word *guru* is freely and casually used, causing much confusion and many misunderstandings. By using the term *guru* for anyone from whom we may have learned something, the profundity of the essential role of the guru—the one with the power to transform and transcend neuroses—is lost. Therefore, again, this vast topic requires careful reflection and understanding.

Guru by Definition

The Sanskrit word *guru* is actually two words: *gu* and *ru*. In Sanskrit, *gu* means "darkness," and *ru* means "light," so *guru* means "someone who illuminates that darkness," or someone with the capacity and ability to cut through the darkness of ignorance. The Tibetan for "guru" is *lama*, which is also two words: *la* and *ma*. *La* means "high" or "elevated," as in "one who has wisdom and pure qualities," and *ma* means "someone with the quality of great kindness." A *lama* refers to one with unsurpassable kindness, or compassion, and the wisdom that can cut through whatever hesitations and doubts you might have. In this way, a lama can help you realize your inherent true potential to a degree that even you, yourself, could not have imagined.

For a student on the path of Dharma, understanding the meaning of *lama*, or *guru*, requires an understanding of the qualities of the guru and the qualities of the student as well. Ultimately, the meaning of *guru* requires both the student and the guru to be true to these qualities, thus allowing them to support and take to fruition the student's journey to enlightenment.

Along the way, of course, you may learn and benefit from many wonderful beings, who undoubtedly would also be gurus in a sense. And there must be deep appreciation for all these teachers, lecturers, and countless clever, smart, helpful, and kind people who act as teachers in our lives. But someone who has that most crucial quality of being able to guide you to bring about absolute enlightenment—and to instill in you the courage to withstand all habitual neuroses—is rare. This is the guru we are talking about here. This is what we mean by a true spiritual friend.

In the Buddhist teachings, especially the Vajrayana teachings, a guru can be defined in three general ways: the outer guru, inner guru, and the secret guru. The outer guru refers to all the teachers from whom one receives teachings, transmissions, guidance, and, ultimately, pith and profound instructions. It is the outer guru who introduces you to the view of Dharma. The inner guru is about taking to the path the view that is pointed out by the outer guru. Therefore, the inner guru refers to the path of the practice of Dharma. With an understanding of the view, one can engage on the path with courage. With clear contemplation of the view, there is the arising of wisdom. When the wisdom that arises from taking the view to the path awakens you to your own true fundamental nature, this is called "meeting the secret guru." Since your fundamental true nature is your own, this ultimate guru is not outside of you but inherent within you.

Now, if this is so, you might ask, "Do I really need an outer guru?" Since the inner guru has to do with your own practice path and the secret guru has to do with your innate basic nature—and since both are up to you and within you—it would seem that there is no need to rely on an outer guru. Essentially, you could simply work on your own with your own nature.

Realistically speaking, however, how many of us can do that? We may have the capacity, but how many of us are even aware of our inherent enlightened nature, let alone are practicing to realize it? Because of our inability to do this on our own, the guidance of an outer guru from whom we receive all the teachings and transmissions is immensely helpful. Most importantly, the outer guru from whom we receive the introduction to our innate primordial buddha nature is crucial.

Generally, when people speak of a guru, it is this outer guru they are referring to. And all the ideas you may have about a guru—finding or not finding a guru, the greatness of the guru, the gurus you have problems with—are very much about this outer guru. The person who does meet with a guru—a guru from whom one receives great knowledge and wisdom, transmissions, empowerments, pith instructions, and practices; a guru endowed with all the disciplines and qualities that must be present in a teacher; and above all, a guru who is patient and truly compassionate—is very fortunate indeed. Within the Nyingma and Kagyu lineages, to be the recipient of the incredible kindness and wisdom of such an outer guru is considered one of the most essential qualities for walking the path to enlightenment.

What Is Devotion?

Someone fortunate enough to meet with a guru endowed with all the qualities of wisdom, compassion, and skillful means must realize that this relationship is beyond emotional likes and dislikes, agreeing and disagreeing, belief and disbelief. It must also be free of attachment and blind faith. Therefore, the word *devotion* must be properly understood.

The definition of the word *devotion* in English seems to point toward a sense of loyalty and love. When used within a spiritual context, it seems to call for surrender, trust, and love. But, if one examines carefully, most of these words emphasize a certain emotion.

In Tibetan, the word for "devotion" is *depa*. Simply translated, *depa* means "confidence" or "deep faith." But *depa* has two characteristics: *mogu* and *yiche*. The first characteristic, *mogu*, consists of two words: *mo*, which means "inspired devotion," and *gu*, which means respect. Therefore, *mogu* refers to being so inspired and humbled by a person's indisputable truth and qualities that ego lays down its defenses. The second characteristic of depa is *yiche*, which is usually translated as "confidence" and also consists of two words: *yi*, meaning "mind," and *che*, which implies something intense. Simply put, *yiche* refers to the mind when struck by something so intense that its power cuts through the usual banter of our habitual neurosis. These are the characteristics of the confidence and deep faith that is devotion.

Devotion within the context of Dharma is not really an expression of emotion nor does it entail a kind of surrender to someone or something. Devotion is seeing someone who has the unquestionable brilliance that illuminates the darkness of all ignorance, someone who has indisputable, unsurpassable, and infinite qualities of wisdom and compassion and who sees within you a capacity that is far beyond what you imagine your limitations to be.

True devotion, or depa, is to experience the guru's truth and qualities so directly that its power cuts through all of one's neurotic deceptions and defenses and thus brings about not only inspiration and humility but also strong confidence within oneself. Such a pure relationship does not, of course, happen overnight. It is a process that comes with time, from receiving teachings, from being with the teacher, from service, and from taking the practices to heart and accomplishing them honestly and genuinely.

CONTEMPLATION

Many teachings emphasize the way in which the student examines the guru and the guru examines the student. In examining a guru, you must look for the incredible quality that has the power to humble your ego in a gentle way, but also the quality of presence that does not allow the ego to find a hiding place. You must find kindness and a brilliance of wisdom that inspires you to emulate these qualities. And most importantly, you must find that this kindness and wisdom allow you to find these qualities within yourself, thus giving you the confidence to manifest them naturally.

THE QUALITIES OF A TEACHER

Always aspire and strive to have the merit to be able to meet a great teacher.

Sometimes I think that if I had just died a few years earlier in my last life, perhaps I would have had the karma to be born a little earlier. This might have given me the opportunity to have more time with some of the greatest teachers of Vajrayana Buddhism of the twentieth century. Still, I am very grateful to have met and received teachings from some of these most precious and wonderful teachers. And it is truly unfortunate that our younger generation of practitioners never had the opportunity to meet with them. Having said that, many wonderful teachers are still teaching today, and I encourage you to aspire and strive to have the merit to meet a teacher from whom you can receive teachings and gain the confidence to tame your mind.

The Buddha's main approach for conveying profound instructions was through personal connection: person to person, teacher to student. These teachings are commonly referred to as *sutras*, a Sanskrit word often translated as "discourses." In *The Discourse Requested by Maitreya*, the Buddha says,

> Any liberation that is gained by a hearer, a solitary realizer, a bodhisattva, or a buddha arises from reliance on a spiritual guru. Moreover, any measure of help or happiness that sentient beings experience arises from the root of our noble actions, which also arise from the spiritual guides.

Reflecting on this quote brings insight into the importance of connecting with a teacher, who will enhance and support one's practice on the path to liberation.

Through receiving teachings, transmissions, vows, and empowerments, your connection to the teacher may be on many different levels. Buddhist practitioners may have many different teachers over the course of their lives. Or, they may receive all the different forms of teachings and transmissions from a single teacher, who may also be their "root teacher." This is the teacher from whom they receive the pith instructions and the introduction to the nature of mind, as well as the blessings to be able to directly experience this.

It is important that whatever one's connection to a teacher or teachers may be, that it be cultivated slowly, with clarity, examination, and knowledge, especially with respect to the Vajrayana teachings. As a Buddhist continues to study, practice, and gain more clarity, they slowly examine the qualities of these teachers to see with whom they connect with more deeply, and whom they might consider to be their guru.

Twelve Analogies for the Guru

In *The Pattern of the Stem Discourse*, the Buddha gives twelve analogies for such a guru:

> Since the guru frees us from the ocean of samsara, the teacher is like a great vessel.
> Since the guru shows us the path of freedom, the teacher is like a guide.
> Since the guru allows us to be rid of nonvirtue, the teacher is like a wish-fulfilling jewel.
> Since the guru extinguishes the fire of karma and mental affliction, the guru is like a river.
> Since the guru causes the torrential rain of profound wisdom, the guru is like excellent clouds.
> Since the guru brings joy to all sentient beings, the guru is like the mighty divine drum.

Since the guru cures one from afflictive emotions, the guru is like a skillful physician.

Since the guru dispels the darkness of ignorance, the guru is like a lamp.

Since the guru fulfills all hopes and desires, the guru is like a wish-fulfilling tree.

Since the guru is imbued with boundless love, the guru is like the sun.

Since the guru brings ease to one's mind, the guru is like the beautiful moon.

Since the guru inspires and encourages a wealth of positive qualities within one, the guru is like Vaishravana, the god of wealth.

These days, the question of how to find a teacher and how to know who is your teacher is very common among Tibetan Buddhists. It is helpful, therefore, to know and reflect on these twelve qualities that a teacher must embody. In general, what is most important is to take the time to study and learn with a teacher. As a student studies and relates to a particular teacher, they may begin to see some or all of these twelve qualities in this individual. Or they might be fortunate enough to relate to several teachers, each of whom has qualities that inspire them. People often ask if you can have many teachers. Absolutely! In today's times, it is very important to open yourself up to studying and learning from those teachers who do embody these qualities.

Students may also come across teachers or people in Buddhist communities, or sanghas, who have very strict ideas about loyalty to a teacher. The word *loyalty* is actually misleading here and can be misused, as has so often occurred within spiritual organizations. In the context of Dharma, the relationship between the teacher and student is about the teacher showing the path that frees one from samsara and the student working wholeheartedly for that. Since this is the focus of the student and the teacher, this relationship has more to do with confidence than loyalty.

In any other context, the relationship with a teacher is very simple: the student learns and is grateful. But in the context of Dharma, the teacher is like a boat, like a wish-fulfilling tree or wish-fulfilling jewel, like a cloud, and so on. The relationship is one of affection, respect, and gratitude.

Essential versus Institutional Buddhism

The teachings of the Buddhadharma and its philosophy are true and pure. However, one must also remember that even the purest form of teachings is taught and practiced by human beings living within this world. The influence of countries and their cultures, and the political and socioeconomic influences on any philosophy are therefore inevitable. In this context, it is helpful to learn a bit about the history of the countries and cultures in which institutional Buddhism evolved.

Buddhism began in India, a powerful civilization with a very profound and rich cultural and religious heritage. Through the centuries, the teachings of the Buddha migrated and flourished in many countries throughout Asia. In the twentieth century, these profound teachings came to the West, where they have flourished these last many decades and were widely taught to millions of Buddhists throughout Europe, North America, and other Western countries. And just as the various Asian cultures influenced the ways in which Buddhism was taught and practiced in the East, Western culture will also affect how the teachings of the Buddha are taught and practiced in the West.

For those who feel inspired by the teachings of the Buddha and for those who practice them, it is important to keep working to connect to the basic core essence of these teachings and, as much as possible, disengage from what may be purely cultural, political, and socioeconomic influences. It is imperative that we recognize how many of these influences are the result of particular cultural or historic needs of the time. Seen in this way, we might even appreciate how these influences could be viewed as skillful means to help establish and expand the teachings in a particular place and time.

Such influences, however, have a temporary use. Not knowing

them to be conditional developments of a particular time and place, one could become fascinated by them and fixate on them alone. Mistaking them to be Dharma will bring more confusion than clarity. This is something that those on the path must examine and reflect upon very carefully.

When the distinction between essential Dharma and the overlay of temporary conditions is not clearly recognized, systems evolve that may be useful at the time but then become mere institutionalized practices. If and when such practices are mistaken for Dharma, one may easily become trapped in systematic dogma, even when the intention is to simply connect with the Buddha's teachings.

For example, you might read that it is prohibited to wear any type of head covering while receiving teachings. This rule came about at a time when kings and high-ranking ministers would attend teachings and big Dharma gatherings. Crowns and parasols were symbols of strength and power in those days and were often a means of showing off one's importance and wealth. This led to pride, jealousy, ostentatiousness, and one-upmanship, which was counterproductive to creating a sacred space. And so it became a rule that head coverings, parasols, and umbrellas were not to be worn or carried during teachings. This was a means to encourage the development of humility, to leave the trappings of wealth and power behind and receive the teachings on an equal basis, along with everyone else gathered in the assembly.

Today, many think that not wearing a hat or head covering while receiving a teaching is a rule, without knowing the actual reason that led to the creation of such a rule. I have seen people receiving teachings and transmissions in sweltering sun, still refusing to cover their heads or use an umbrella for shade because they think it would somehow be disrespectful. Of course, it would be far more practical to cover one's head and protect oneself from sunstroke than to blindly follow a rule. This is a good example of how a rule that once served the beneficial purpose of creating a peaceful, respectful teaching environment for the assembly might not be necessary for people attending a teaching today.

How does one determine whether a practice is essential Dharma or institutional Dharma? To make this determination, one must know what essential Dharma is, as opposed to mere institutionalized practices. This requires some in-depth study and knowledge of the Dharma and its historical origins and practices. For those wishing to connect to the Buddhadharma, therefore, it is very important to take the time and make a genuine effort to gain some knowledge about it.

Often, there is the general notion that spirituality is about inspiration, about the truth, about having deep faith—and so it is not really necessary to learn and study much. There are those who place more importance on the "heart" aspect of Dharma and who have a certain reluctance toward study. On the other hand, there are the intellectuals who are very keen about the study of Buddhist philosophy, even to the detriment of practice and true realization. Neither of these approaches is the best one. In order to understand and benefit from Buddhadharma, a balanced and genuine approach to study and practice is imperative.

Knowledge is important. To acquire knowledge about the various aspects of practice and the philosophy of Buddhadharma, through hearing the teachings, studying extensively, engaging in deep reflection, contemplation, and examination is especially important. These activities allow you to know the true intent and meaning of the teachings. Especially in the context of Vajrayana teachings and practices, knowledge and understanding of meaning and symbolism is even more crucial. In order to engage in Vajrayana practices as they were intended, for example, the meaning of lineage, rituals, modes of meditation, and symbolic icons must be known and understood. These are some things to consider carefully when determining essential Dharma and, most importantly, when contemplating the role of a teacher on the path of practice.

What Else to Be Careful About?

When determining what is essential Dharma, one must carefully consider what the essential role of the teacher is on this path. As mentioned earlier, the relationship you build with a teacher must not carry the same emotional stickiness that you find in mundane relationships within samsara. In particular, look out for the tendency to befriend your teacher. Because most relationships in the mundane world are built on emotions and feelings, such relationships involve many expectations, hopes, and fears. When you seek to relate to a teacher in the same way, things can get very complicated because ego gets involved—and most importantly, such complications could cause you to distance yourself from the true essential Dharma.

This is why the teacher-student relationship is not something to enter into lightly. If you do not examine carefully those involved in the relationship, and what the relationship is truly about, it could be detrimental to your path of practice. So rather than jumping into a teacher-student relationship in a starry-eyed manner, take careful, thoughtful steps toward finding a teacher, whom you might then see as your guru.

I sometimes feel that Buddhists invest much more time and care in looking for the right partner and examining their samsaric relationships than they do in searching for a teacher. Yet the teacher-student relationship can have long-term consequences, both good and bad. Therefore, it must be undertaken with utmost care, and with the discerning wisdom that examines the qualities of a teacher to see whether this is a person who can provide you with the guidance you need, and not simply the guidance you want. To apply a mundane approach to a relationship that should actually free you from dualistic concepts and fixations, you would end up living a paradox, when instead you could be cultivating the true view beyond dualistic fixations.

This misunderstanding is often accentuated by the term *spiritual friend*, which is a translation of the Tibetan *geweshenyen*. In Tibetan, *gewa* is often translated as "virtue," and *shenyen* means "friend." This can be misunderstood to mean your friend on the spiritual path—which is not what it means. The term *shenyen* refers to someone who encourages you on the path of virtue, or simply "a friend of virtue." The spiritual friend is someone who inspires you to walk the path of virtue.

This term *virtue* must also be carefully understood. The Tibetan term *gewa*, or "virtue," refers to the inner strength of your awareness, which arouses in you the confidence to go beyond delusion. Acting with virtue results in behaviors that serve more as agents of good than agents of discursiveness. Thus, a spiritual friend is someone who would not cater to any preconceived notions, attachments, or other discursive delusions.

Perhaps you think you want a guru with whom you can sit down in a bar and share a drink. That may sound nice, down-to-earth, or more "real." In today's day and age, many strive to make the Dharma relatable in just such a mundane manner. But why would you want to do that to the sublime Dharma? Dharma is "real" in the sense that it doesn't have to be this way or that. Dharma is just Dharma—beyond having to make you feel comfortable or uncomfortable, at ease or in awe. The magnificence and excellence of Dharma lie in the very fact that it is beyond needing to be a certain way or to fit into certain mundane concepts.

When you meet a true teacher of Dharma—someone with genuine qualities, who is learned and accomplished, and who inspires within you the potential of true liberation—this is indeed a rare and wonderful opportunity that must be treasured.

CONTEMPLATION

If the teacher you are relying upon for liberation from samsaric suffering and delusion is no better than a friend who supports you in your limitations—just as emotional, needy, and confused as you are, with the same tendencies of grasping to hope and fear—be careful. That would be like going out to sea in a boat with a captain who doesn't know how to navigate the waters. It might not be the wisest thing to do.

Study and reflect on the qualities that must be present in a teacher and a student. Then be careful in selecting your captain. Choose a captain who really knows the waters, and who knows all the best routes and dangers along the way.

Beyond Indulgence, Entertainment, and Answers

In general, a Buddhist teacher must be kind and patient with students, but this does not mean indulging the student's neuroses. As for the student, you have the support of the teachings and instructions on what to do and what not to do—but you are never really given all the answers. In this way, you are encouraged to make the experience of the truth of the teachings your own. This builds your confidence in seeing truth as a direct experience. It is the responsibility of a true teacher—without in any way entertaining you, sustaining your ego, or indulging your confusion—to let this realization build to a crescendo.

A teacher who hands you a glass of water every time you are thirsty will lead you to believe that water is the solution. This would make you a believer, and beliefs can be very fragile. If you get a little more water than the others, your belief increases; a little less, and you begin to wonder if the teacher is paying more attention to them than to you, which immediately causes more confusion. You should know, therefore, that the teacher in your life will be someone who makes sure—through teachings, practices, and various examples—not to indulge you or provide any entertainment.

For anyone fortunate enough to have met with the Dharma in this life, it is a tremendous advantage to meet a teacher with these qualities. Such a teacher will provide strong support and guidance for experiencing the teachings directly and, through this realization, for becoming absolutely and totally independent of the teacher. In the end, this is the best result from a student-teacher relationship. As a result of the teacher's guidance, the student experiences truth directly and, through this realization, becomes independent of any teacher. This is the best gift a teacher can give you; this is the best gift you can receive from a teacher. When blessings and one's merit come to fruition as an opportunity to be with such a teacher, this is a chance students must learn not to miss.

THE QUALITIES OF A STUDENT

In the sutras, the Buddha says to Ananda, "Transcendent buddhas do not appear to all sentient beings, but spiritual guides do appear to all beings. They bestow the profound Dharma and plant the seed of liberation." It is for this reason that a fortunate student of Dharma owes more gratitude to one's spiritual master than even to a transcendent buddha. It is for this reason that one should engage with such a teacher with strong devotion and respect.

The adorning quality of strong devotion is to be without discouragement and fatigue. If you have ever been with a teacher, you know there are times when discouragement and impatience can envelop your mind, often for no reason at all. On a good day, you think it is inspiring to meditate; on a bad day, you just feel very sorry about being where you are, and you allow your mind to be caught in doubt and fear. Instead of being driven or overtaken by such tendencies, it is important to remain diligent and patient with yourself and others as well. Most importantly, remain on guard against those deceptive tendencies that encourage and support the ego and habitual neurosis. Without the basic qualities of diligence and patience, you will remain untouched by the teachings and guidance that come from a teacher.

Devotion—to the teachings, to the path of practice, to the teacher—is the antidote to habitual tendencies of discouragement and fear. Genuine devotion gives rise to genuine joy. It awakens a deep sense of appreciation for your path of practice, and an almost indescribable feeling of joyous wonder at the unfurling of your own innate buddha nature. Therefore, there is every reason to cultivate the qualities of diligence, patience, and honesty and no reason to try to deceive a teacher or oneself or to try to live up to any other expectations.

That Sparkly Thing We Do

People tend to deceive themselves when relating to the guru, even though there is no need to conceal from themselves or anyone else who they naturally are. There is no need to get lost in spiritual melodrama, no need to pretend to be something you are not, no use pretending to be super profound or to make extra effort to be noticed. Nothing is more bothersome than getting lost in this kind of spiritual drama. Instead of the direct path, you are taking the long way around.

Sometimes when there is a gathering around a teacher, I look around the room and joke about that sparkly thing that some people do. There is no other way to explain it. When such a drama is taking place, their eyes sparkle, and their bodies begin to shift in ways that display ego's need for attention. This is the time to keep in mind the many ways we deceive ourselves. There is no need to try to cultivate some kind of outward spark or some form of artifice to live up to expectations of how a yogi-type or a great scholar should be. What is most important to cultivate is the light of our own innate nature. This is what could just naturally light up the entire three thousand realms, without any need of ostentatious demonstrations of an inner spark. Otherwise—an act is just an act, and at some point, it must come to an end.

There is a famous saying in Tibetan: "When you store ordinary wood among sandalwood, the ordinary wood takes on the sandalwood fragrance." Agreed! But that is not the whole saying. The other half says, "When you take the ordinary wood away from the sandalwood, it's just ordinary wood." So this is for all the sparkly, dramatic students who try to draw on the energy of the teachers by simply being around them: Deceiving yourself and deceiving the teacher—nothing comes of it.

THE JOURNEY BEGINS

When a student has the courage to cultivate the qualities of honesty, humor, patience, humility, and diligence, they begin a beautiful journey of self-discovery and the unearthing of the tremendous inherent qualities of their basic human nature. With an open mind, discipline, and flexibility, you begin to learn and reflect on the meaning and intent of the enlightened ones, and you learn to appreciate the boundless extent of your own buddha nature: awakened basic goodness. The possibility of this discovery being realized is made more accessible if you are fortunate enough to meet with a truly qualified teacher. The meeting of a teacher and student with pure qualities sets one on the path, and thus the journey begins.

The realization of your beautiful inherent potential has all the possibilities of becoming the basis of great goodness and happiness for yourself and others. This is marvelous. In today's times, we all have an even greater responsibility to put effort into cultivating this intrinsic goodness and sanity. As human beings, we have this potential and therefore the responsibility to deepen this recognition. Through the realization of your own potential, you have the possibility to be, if not a perfect example, then at least an inspiration to others.

So please do your best. Make the impact of your sincere effort on this path manifest your true nature and in this way bring together the basis of sanity and happiness for countless sentient beings. This journey—which is not made "out there" but within you—is simple and powerful, should you simply choose to begin. Whether or not you consider yourself Buddhist, if you do see value in the teachings of Dharma, this should be your view and your path.

SIX

The Heartbeat of Dharma

WHAT MAKES THE BUDDHIST perspective different from other religious or philosophical perspectives is its combination of direct experience with analysis or careful examination. When the Buddha examined his own experience, he saw four things to be true. He saw the truth of impermanence. He saw that suffering is caused by contaminated, or afflicted, emotions. He saw that all things are empty in nature. And he saw that there is, in fact, enlightenment, or peace. This insight and understanding is known as the Four Seals. When we undertake to examine and contemplate these fundamental subjects, we are essentially doing what the Buddha himself did.

The Four Seals are the basic pillars of Buddhadharma. Basically, they designate what it means to be a Buddhist—which does not mean that one blindly accepts these four truths. Being a Buddhist means that you have received teachings on the Four Seals, that you understand what they are pointing toward, that you have contemplated them, and that, having examined them for yourself, you have found them to be true. If the result of your contemplation and analysis is that the Four Seals accurately describe how you view the world—this is what it means to be a Buddhist. What do you do as a Buddhist? You live and breathe this perspective.

ALL COMPOUNDED THINGS
ARE IMPERMANENT

The first thing to be understood by a living, breathing Buddhist is the impermanence of all compounded things. The term *compounded* refers back to interdependence. Everything that comes into being is dependent on the coming together of temporary causes and conditions, all of which change, evolve, and are by nature empty, or not solid. Thus, all compounded things—all physical forms, perceptions, and movements of mind—are impermanent. At the moment of death, they must all be left behind. It is from this perspective that you would relate to all occurrences: all feelings, thoughts, and experiences, good or bad. Whatever else you might think a Buddhist does every day, an acute awareness of impermanence is imperative. This is the first seal.

The truth of impermanence may not be new to you, but the mind may stubbornly refute it. To cut through any stubborn belief in a reality or truth that is permanent, you can rely on the razor-sharp wisdom of the great Nagarjuna, father of the Madhyamaka teachings of Mahayana Buddhism, and his disciple Aryadeva. These teachings encourage us to examine the seemingly permanent, unchanging, intransient appearance of things. Countless examples are dissected—physical pots, vases, and the pillars of buildings; minute particles and molecules; and subjective labels and objects of mind, including time—to reveal their emptiness nature. It is through the understanding of the impermanent and empty nature of things that Buddhism came to be known as the middle way.

This same understanding is more gently conveyed using the change of seasons and times of day. I change, you change; he died, she died—but what do we do with this knowledge? We take good notes and nod our heads with tremendous respect because who can argue with that? Then we go back to doing things from an entirely different perspective. If you truly understood the preciousness of this life and the indisputable truth of Dharma, you wouldn't waste time being a Buddhist in name only. There would occur within you a gradual change steeped in the confidence of seeing the impermanence of things as they are.

As a young girl growing up with monks—with the exception of my mother and sister, Jetsunla—I was stubborn and headstrong. I became known as someone who was often difficult to deal with. If today I do not come across this way as much, it may be just due to physically aging. It takes a lot of energy to be stubborn and obstinate.

At times when I would get very wound up, everyone around me would be faced with this person who seemed to refuse to budge. They would try to come up with creative ways to deal with me and to make me fit more into the norm. This was especially difficult, as I was seen as a sort of rare species, like a rare breed of mouse that you had to be really careful with lest it become extinct. It was really just another mouse—but this mouse had a certain title, sat on a throne, and happened to be female. This was a rather rare species.

So when this rare mouse got stubborn and difficult to handle, obviously the lives of those around me became difficult. How do you handle a rare but difficult mouse? How do you handle a person like that? Even more difficult was the life of my teacher, who was also my father. Looking back—and I say this sincerely—things must have been frustrating for him at times. When I got very wound up, I could react explosively to certain situations and remain unbudging behind what I thought to be right.

One day my teacher called for me. "Today," he said, "I'm going to give you a mantra to recite whenever you feel things are getting really wound up. Just say to yourself, 'This too will pass.'" Now, we have all heard this before, so I didn't take it very seriously at the time. But as time went by, I would reflect upon it whenever something occurred that might have caused me to get wound up. And more and more, it became an important practice. Today, it helps me tremendously. As I grow older—having spent thirty years telling people what to do and observing how often they don't do it—it helps me to relax. This too will pass.

This is the view of impermanence. It is extremely important for those of us who take everything we do, especially with regards to spirituality, way more seriously than is necessary. Often, the kindest thing one can do for others and oneself is to give some space. Give space to just breathe, to let things unfold and play out to the fullest of their capacity and then get exhausted. Give space to know that it's okay, even when not everything is okay, because everything is transient. This too shall pass. And because everything moves on, every moment that arises and touches our lives is precious in its own way.

Dharma becomes very burdensome when we are trying to be so selfless, so good, so patient, so enlightened, and so kind that we almost explode with the deliberateness of this effort. Knowing that this moment is impermanent, we could just let things pass by. Then we wouldn't need to read about patience to be patient or try to posture ourselves into our primordial nature. Then we could love others for who and what they are and forgive them more easily. We would be a bit happier with what we already have—and most importantly, we would come to treasure a little more humor in life.

We Buddhists tend to make so many things very important. There seem to be so many things that we need in order to lessen self-cherishing and self-absorption. We need a good teacher, good teachings, good retreat places, and the time to do a retreat. We need the understanding of others. We need the answers to all of our very good questions. And of course, we need practices, liturgies, and people to explain them—and we need for all of these demands to be met.

When we think that everything must be given to us, that only then will this path be possible, the idea of actually giving up or letting go is difficult. It is much easier to give up and let go when we have very little to start with. But we tend to solidify our expectations, along with our thoughts, emotions, and experiences. In this effort to freeze things, delusion sets in, and we forget that all compounded things are impermanent.

Selfies Won't Freeze the Moment

The selfie culture is a good example of trying to freeze what is impermanent. Most of our selfies are just a big head in a frame. Even so, we try to freeze the moment—and we do so with an immense sense of hope. Now, where there is immense hope, fear is not far behind. So don't do that. Take it from me: trying to freeze every moment to conform to your wishes is a painful thing to do to yourself.

This life is subject to destruction. As fragile and vulnerable as a bubble of water or a candle flame in the wind, it can be interrupted in billions of ways. Time slips away, and every breath that you take reduces the amount of time you have left. So as Milarepa taught, there is no time to waste. Recognize change at every moment: changes in your inner feelings and emotions, physical changes, changes in the environment, seasonal changes, changes in all your relationships. And hold the view that all compounded things are impermanent.

This is what a Buddhist does. Whether or not you study or do visualizations and mantras is secondary. Whether you are a Vajrayanist, Mahayanist, or even a Buddhist is secondary. The primary thing is to keep the perspective of impermanence. This is the first seal. All compounded things are impermanent.

CONTEMPLATION

Take time to really contemplate, examine, and experience directly what is meant by "things change." Ponder all aspects of your life in this way. The natural outcome of this pondering will allow you to relax with yourself and with your world. When your attitude is more relaxed, everything that you are trying to learn—how to meditate, how to be kind, how to be more patient and more mindful—will result automatically.

ALL CONTAMINATED EMOTIONS ARE PAINFUL

The second seal requires that you constantly observe and examine your inability to free others from yourself.

The second seal is sometimes translated as "All emotions are suffering," or "All that is contaminated is painful." Both refer to the pain caused by emotions that are contaminated, or tainted, by self-absorption. The Tibetan word for this kind of contamination is *zagche*: the contamination that gives birth to afflicted, or disturbing, emotions.

The five primary afflicted emotions, called *kleshas* in Sanskrit, are ignorance, desire, anger, jealousy, and pride. We don't usually count the sixth afflictive emotion, which is doubt. But when it comes to seeing things clearly, the vacillating momentum of doubt is said to be the greatest hindrance. The root of all doubt is a lack of faith, or trust, in the extraordinary power of the human mind. From the point of view of meditation, this could be seen as "afflicted awareness." There is awareness; there is *shepa*, or "consciousness," and there is clarity. But that awareness, rather than trusting its own basic nature and resting in that, is persuaded by the momentum of seeing something else to move toward, to discern and interpret. Thus, awareness becomes afflicted with self-absorption and all its demands.

With the demanding attitude of self-absorption, nothing has the freedom to simply be what it is. Not a moment and nothing arising in any moment are free to arise on their own, without having to conform to our interpretation—which is the exact opposite of bodhichitta, or kindness. This is what is meant by taint, or contamination. The second seal requires that you watch your emotions, and constantly examine your inability to free others from yourself.

There Is Nothing Wrong with Emotions, but . . .

Emotions are rampant, and there is nothing wrong with them. But we unnecessarily contaminate, or color, our feelings to become tools of ego's demands. With what do we color our emotions? We color them with assumptions. It wouldn't be so bad if we colored emotions with facts. The problem is, we color them with assumptions based on hope and fear, delusions and suppositions. We then map out our lives and views based on these assumptions, which are a cause of nothing but suffering for others and ourselves. Like any bad habit of self-harm, this is the pain of contaminated emotions.

If you were willing to work with this tendency to manipulate feelings and emotions, there would be no need to practice anything called kindness or compassion—other than the kindness of letting each moment arise free of your demands and free of the "makeup" you apply on it. If nothing else, you would end up with more time on your hands. Look carefully and see, for example, that when you're feeling overworked and exhausted, it is not necessarily your work that's tiring you out. Exhaustion comes from interfering in things that don't need your interference.

In the Tibetan Buddhist tradition, there are practices like the three-year retreat, which, among other things, let you know that everything is just fine without you. The whole world functions without your interference. And what did you think meditation was about? You sit still, nothing happens, and it is not catastrophic. You keep quiet. Everything is okay. You let your mind rest. Everyone is happy. These practices are about reorienting the mind to stop coloring and contaminating everything the senses perceive.

What do you do then? You do what we all do: you see, hear, speak, smell, have tactile sensations and a very vivid mind—without making a big deal of them. No need to get into the habit of writing about every passing experience and how it was or wasn't up to the mark or how it was so fantastic that you must do it again. These are the variables we bring in that taint the senses. Instead, you should know that with uncontaminated, or absolute, awareness, you can create your own realms of experience. That hell realm is something you create; the realm of nirvana is also your creation.

It is said that in the latter part of his life, the great master Jamyang Khyentse Wangpo, an absolutely realized teacher, was found to be prostrating in odd places. One time it was a little too much: he was found prostrating to a water pump. His attendants tried to cover this up lest it be misunderstood. You don't want your teacher, the great master, to be seen as a senile person prostrating to a water pump. They tried to tell him to stop. But when they asked him what he thought he was doing prostrating to a water pump, Jamyang Khyentse Wangpo replied, "Wherever I look is a buddha field. I could prostrate here, there, or anywhere. Why not prostrate to a water pump?" There is a lot to learn from this example, and it's not about prostrating to plumbing. It is about a Buddhist view of what is good and what is bad, who is right and who is wrong—beyond your mind's creation of it. What is here or there, what is beautiful or ugly, beyond your mind's creation?

Because your very creative mind can color anything—any form, sound, or thought—when you talk about compassion, you are talking about relaxing your attitude and freeing others from you. Most things are not under your control in any case, so you can just relax with the nature of change. Within that relaxation—because you do understand the creative potential of your mind and the responsibility that comes with it—work to not contaminate whatever arises.

This is the logic of Buddhist ethics. It comes not from a dogmatic, fatalistic, or pessimistic perspective. It comes from a natural awareness of our responsibility for others, knowing that our mind is the basis of limitless kinds of productions. Awareness of the responsibility that we share with all beings brings sanity into our lives. Since everything is colored by mind, may your mind not color so busily; but if you must, make sure you color things well or not at all. This is the meaning of the second seal.

ALL PHENOMENA ARE EMPTY

The third seal is the emptiness nature of everything. As our great teachers would say, beyond our common consensus, what is the reality of anything but a temporary display of interdependence and simple functionality?

An area of study in the Tibetan monastic system is grammar, which we studied using a dictionary called *Lamp of Speech*. My grammar teacher was very diligent about traditional ways of learning. This basically began with memorizing the dictionary: the words, their synonyms, and their meanings. I never saw the point of this. I was also in a modern school system at the time, and a dictionary was something you had on your desk in case you needed it. But my Tibetan teacher never gave up, so I memorized the dictionary. Today, the only thing I remember is the first phrase, "*Karmapa ni trinlepa*," meaning "*Karmapa* means 'one who engages in activity,'" which is like learning "*A* is for apple." I mention this because we all grow up learning dictionaries: dictionaries of words and concepts, about which we have common consensus—or bones of contention—as we try to solidify our world.

My Egg, Not Yours

When my sister Jetsunla's two children, Dungse Rinpoche and Jetsun Rinpoche, were babies, I learned a lot about how we teach concepts to small children. For example, my niece and nephew liked eggs, and I too liked to have an egg for breakfast. Because I needed to get on with the various activities of the day, their eggs were served a bit later than mine. And in this situation, I found myself teaching them the concept of my egg: "Egg—but this one not for you," and "This is my egg."

We instill these concepts of "yours" and "mine" to try to solidify things. And we are very good at it; with such concepts and labels, we bring solidification to everything. It is the precious teachings and the kindness of our great teachers that allow us to analyze this conceptual reality and see the truth of emptiness.

The Madhyamaka teachings, as I mentioned before, investigate things down to the minutest of particles and time itself in order to demolish any belief in the solidity and permanence of compounded phenomena. Now, when these profound teachings were traditionally taught in India and Tibet, they had to work through the strong theistic view of the people. Therefore, the examples used in the texts—pillars, pots, chariots, and so on—were designed for the understanding and references of that time. The modern mind of today has a keener ability to analyze and examine phenomena in a variety of ways due to broad exposure to modern science and technology.

Having said that, it is not difficult to intellectually comprehend the emptiness nature of things. Both our intellect and our keen innate wisdom already have inklings of this truth. But the sharpness of this mind must still contend with the habit of saying, "This is my egg."

If Anyone Asks

Conditioned from childhood—in this and many lifetimes—our unexamined consensus of belief in labels shapes our lives. It also leads us to imagine that what we say and think is true, real, and permanent. Thus, in spite of life's uncertainty and our inherent understanding of the truth of emptiness, we may not live in accord with this truth. It is essential, therefore, to examine and recognize the fundamental nature of everything we perceive. Then—beyond any superficial study or agreement with Nagarjuna—we can take that as our primary perspective on life.

As the Buddha very simply said in the first turning of the wheel of Dharma, "What is not mind?" and then, "What is mind?" This is the profound pith of the Dharma perspective. It is the core essence of what it means to be a Buddhist. More important and powerful than any practices, any numbers of recitations, or anything else you might do is this contemplation: What is not mind, and what is that mind? This is the basis of your exploration and realization. And if anyone asks, this is what a Buddhist should do.

CONTEMPLATION

In order to train the mind, especially in the Mahamudra and Dzogchen traditions, meditators are advised to ask, "What is the reality of anything?" Take time to look for the reality of anything beyond the perceiving mind.

When you realize that, indeed, all experience is carried in the vast expanse of your own mind, rest in that relaxed state. Then, ponder even more the nature of this mind that is the basis of everything. When you don't find anything— which is usually the case—then you can take a really long break.

NIRVANA IS PEACE

The fourth seal is about being able to exhale. You relax, and relax some more. Relax naturally, relax peacefully. As the Zen masters say: "When you eat, you eat. When you walk, walk. When you have something to do, just do it." This is what a Buddhist does. Nothing changes, yet everything changes because your perspective is very different.

What makes a Buddhist perspective different? Through contemplating the Four Seals, one sees that beyond impermanence, suffering, and the emptiness nature of all things, there is peace. Outwardly, a Buddhist doesn't stand out, but inwardly this view makes you very flexible. On the other hand, if you are always wound up and on a treadmill, after which you need some candyfloss, you may be a good follower of the Buddhist view, but a good follower and a good Buddhist are two different people. I leave the choice up to you.

THE KINDNESS OF THE BUDDHA
WHEN PASSING AWAY

When the Buddha was in his eighties, the question of his successor arose. Who would lead the community when the Buddha passed away? This was widely discussed among the nuns, monks, arhats, bodhisattvas, and others. The most popular choice was Ananda, the Buddha's cousin. Ananda had served the Buddha his entire life, and everyone knew how much the Buddha loved him. Not only was he the Buddha's favorite, he was also an accomplished practitioner. And having never missed one of the Buddha's teachings, he was very learned and well known for his immense capacity to memorize. Everyone in the community took Ananda to be the Buddha's natural heir.

When the time came for the Buddha to announce his successor, the congregation was called together in the area of Vulture's Peak in India. Thousands gathered, and there was a great deal of excitement. It is said that the buzz among the people became increasingly intense because the Buddha was uncharacteristically late that day.

When he finally approached, the Buddha was holding a flower in his hand. Without saying a word, he stood for a long time, looking at everyone. He then sat down for the longest time holding the flower silently. With their eyes fixed eagerly on the Buddha, the people could hardly breathe—everyone except Mahakashyapa, who was very relaxed. Sitting in front of the Buddha, he just lowered his gaze and smiled. And at that moment, the Buddha got up and handed him the flower. Mahakashyapa would be the successor and next lineage holder of the Buddhist tradition.

The people were appalled at the Buddha's decision. Mahakashyapa, while a wonderful practitioner and scholar, was already quite old when he joined the Buddha. The great bodhisattvas Shariputra, Ananda, and the others were much younger and had been with the Buddha for a much longer time. Surely someone who had only recently come into the Buddha's community, someone from a strong Hindu background no less, was not as deserving as their favorite, Ananda. This was the first really great disturbance in the community, and it went on for many months. But after Buddha passed away, there was no retracting his decision.

Mahakashyapa was immediately enthroned as the successor—and his very first decision was to excommunicate Ananda. Now, if you reacted to that, you can imagine the reaction two thousand five hundred years ago. It was then that the first actual schism in Buddhism took place. More than half the nuns and monks left the community. In his biography, Ananda laments having been sent away. Having lost his teacher, he had lost a father to whom he had been wholeheartedly devoted. Then in the physical absence of the Buddha, he had to physically leave the community. He wept. Everybody else wept. And many traveled with him to southern India, where Ananda created his own very large community of devoted students.

What Ananda Then Understood

After a few years, Ananda began to see that his students were doing well. They were getting it—and he was not. He began to feel that he was teaching things he had not experienced. He could teach very well because he had received the teachings very well. But in his writings we find Ananda bereft of the significant transcendence and change, the enlightened awakening, that his students were experiencing. And at that point, he went off to practice diligently.

After some time, there came a day when Ananda awoke. Upon his awakening, he said, "I now understand the immense kindness of the Buddha and, more so, the immense kindness of Mahakashyapa. Had I been chosen as the successor, I never would have practiced the Dharma. I would have led many people and become famous for teaching the Dharma to many followers, but I would have never experienced the truth."

What Mahakashyapa had understood was the Buddha's emphasis on training the mind—and how kind it was for him to take the community's blame for Ananda's excommunication! Had he said to Ananda, "Now that I am the successor, you need to practice," it wouldn't have gone well. Instead, he saw that excommunicating Ananda was the only way for Ananda to come into his own and to understand his own mind. This was the most important thing because working with one's own mind is the only way to realize absolute truth.

The story of Ananda and Mahakashyapa is a wonderful way to understand the view one must have as a Buddhist meditator. This is what Buddhist meditation is about. Ultimately, it doesn't matter which texts you read or which teacher or lineage you have; it doesn't even matter if you're a Buddhist, although that support could be helpful. Likewise, having a teacher and doing various practices could be helpful. Acquiring wisdom and knowledge from the texts is extremely helpful. But they are secondary to squeezing out a better human mind and heart.

All the various tools are meant to illuminate your innate capacity for love, patience, kindness and contentment and to instill trust in your genuine goodness. Then you will reach the point where you can truly say, "I choose to remain with my inherent goodness, and I'll team up with courage to withstand opposing forces—especially the momentum of old habits."

What Not to Underestimate

Viruses come up with ingenious ways to become immune to antidotes. In the same way, we human beings come up with ingenious ways of resisting our innate brilliant wisdom. Our mistrust and doubt in innate goodness—and our habitual trust in anything and everything else—is immense. You cannot underestimate this pull of habitual movement toward "other" and its virus-like resistance to wisdom. You cannot underestimate the web of complications that this pull creates—with its teachers, good and bad; teachings, easy and difficult; hundreds of different methods; and so on.

Sadly, when one gets embroiled in all this, the view of taming and training one's own mind gets lost. This is why spiritual philosophy must be refined to its simplest essence. Buddhism is itself very simple, if you have the courage to stay with the fact of your absolutely true nature. Lacking that trust in your innate goodness, your confidence will weaken. And that's when you will begin to unnecessarily complicate things.

When the belief in "basic badness" becomes stronger than our confidence in basic goodness, we become bogged down struggling with all our inadequacies and complaints. The sense of something lacking makes us susceptible to habitual tendencies, and that's when ego catches and manipulates us. Ordinarily, we may go through life being pretty sure of ourselves—but just when we need a little pride in our basically good nature, ego decides to be humble. What should really humble us is our habitual mistrust. And because two thousand five hundred years ago, people struggled with the same patterns of mistrust and complication, the Buddha was left with no choice but to teach the Dharma in various complex ways.

Someone with a complicated mind and an immense fascination with "other" will find complicated methods helpful. Someone with a less complicated mind will have the good luck to be able to approach the same teachings with more self-reliance. The very fortunate ones are those with a simple mind—simple in the sense of being just the opposite of the popular worldly belief in complicated thinking.

This always surprises me in today's media. It seems that the more complicated people are, the more learned and capable they're seen to be. On TV news networks like CNN, for example, distinguished people wearing ties give their opinions and judgments on various topics: natural disasters, air crashes, bombings. They do have a lot to say, but if you listen from beginning to end, you find they don't actually say anything at all. When asked for their thoughts after a disastrous earthquake in Nepal, which caused so many deaths, they all agreed, "Very bad. We had one before. We might have one again. Don't know when." You don't need a tie and a TV spot for that. It's a good example of our fondness for complication. But what actually comes of it?

With no disrespect to distinguished people who are learned in their own fields, from the perspective of a Buddhist meditator, what's the point? Is the point to be socially responsible by deepening our understanding of the cause of the world's suffering or to acknowledge the basic goodness of this world as our working base? Or are these opinions and judgments dominated by ego's biases and convenience? In this case, they ultimately complicate the mind by either sidestepping or entangling us in the messes we create.

Miracles and Magic Tricks

Our opinions and judgments about appearances are very powerful. From the point of view of cause and effect, they propel karma. The karma we create builds a sphere of experience for ourselves and for the world at large. So, it might be more socially responsible to awaken every day to the simple fact of your wonderful mind as your working base. With trust in your innate goodness, you could choose to simply be a good human being. That would be something for a panel of people to discuss on CNN! In today's world, that would be a true miracle.

When my sister Jetsunla and I were growing up, we would read about the great masters and their miraculous activities. How inspiring it would be to be able to say that our teacher performed miracles! So we asked His Holiness if he could perform miracles like the teachers in the past. Rinpoche just laughed and said, "If that's what interests you, you'd be better off learning magic tricks. Magicians do much better miracles than meditators or yogis." He then added, "The greatest miracle I've done in my life is to have never actually hurt anyone. If you don't think that that's a miracle, then I do not do miracles."

It is not considered an extraordinary achievement to be clairvoyant, or to be able to fly, or to radiate light. But for practitioners to be able to be in samsara without detaching themselves, to be totally mindful of their responsibilities, and to maintain their awareness—that is an extraordinary achievement. That is why, if any kind of realization is to be attained, it will be attained in this world and nowhere else.

CONTEMPLATION

Do not try to escape from this world. Simply be. Don't plan so many things; just work on being aware of this day's actions and this moment's thoughts and attitudes. Have certainty in fundamental human goodness. Certainty is simply the courage to face the truth of your own wisdom mind. Then, instead of miracles or magic tricks, you will have the confidence to allow goodness to be ever present in this world, without becoming entangled in illusory appearances.

SEVEN

Whichever Way
the World Turns

When confidence arises from your own understanding, you are no longer separate from what you understand to be true.

THERE CAME A TIME WHEN the Buddha's students asked him, "How will it be in the future for those who practice your teachings?" In reply, the Buddha is said to have thrown his cup into a flowing river—and the cup floated upstream. Pointing to the cup, the Buddha said, "For people practicing my teachings in the future, it will be as difficult as it is for this cup to float against the current."

THE MEANING OF PRACTICE

Those of us trying to practice the Dharma are going against the current of samsara. Obviously, for a mind attached to samsara, the practice of Buddhadharma will not be convenient. If you're looking for convenience, or temporary relief, or short-term gains, or to satisfy a curious mind, you won't find it. What does it mean then to practice the Dharma?

The word *practice* in this context is a translation of the Tibetan word *nyamlen*. What *nyamlen* actually means is "to follow whatever you have understood to be of value." The expanded meaning is to adopt what you value as your life's path. This is the meaning of practice. It begins with careful thought and reflection. What is the view of this practice that you're about to adopt? What is the value of that? When you understand the meaning of what you are doing, confidence will naturally arise in your mind. Yes, you are aware of habitual patterns. And because the human mind is still stuck with a need for structure and support, you may wonder where to begin or how to go further. But when confidence arises from your own understanding, you are no longer separate from what you understand to be true. Through relying on direct experience and your own wisdom mind, you can put your confidence into action. This is basically what the Buddha did.

WHY WE HAVE TO TALK
ABOUT COURAGE

Imagine you are on your deathbed, struggling for breath, fearful, in pain, and not wanting to die. What would you not give to have life restored? Then imagine a bodhisattva turns up with the nectar of immortality. One sip would relieve your pain and restore your life. The bodhisattva can see that there are just a few drops of nectar left in the vessel, but that should work. You open your mouth— but now the bodhisattva's hand is shaking and those last drops are about to miss.

The point here is that like the nectar of immortality for a dying person, when something is truly important to you, you value and treasure it. Like cool air for someone dying of heat or water for someone dying of thirst, like protection for someone in danger, if you do see value in the teachings of Dharma, this should be your view and your path.

These days, there is often a business-deal relationship to Dharma. Dharma teachings may come at a certain price. There are prices for senior citizens and people with low incomes and scholarships for those who can't pay anything at all. And that's all right. It is relevant to the world we live in; it is nothing to interfere with. But putting a price on the teachings can impact the way we relate to Dharma. For example, when you go to the theater and you really enjoy the show, you feel you got your money's worth. When you bring this same attitude to the teachings, you want to get something that's worth what you paid for it—and you want to get something you like. Whether or not you think this way doesn't matter; that thought has dropped into today's psyche. And with that kind of business-deal approach to Dharma, the teachings won't be valued like the last drops of the nectar of immortality.

If I were on my deathbed and someone asked, "What is your biggest complaint about all the students in your life?" first on the list would be their tendency to pick and choose which teachings they like. In the West, this is probably influenced by a very individualistic lifestyle. But today, East and West, many people have a very stylish way of practicing the Dharma, with very particular likes and dislikes, and a love of convenience.

A mind that seeks convenience spends its days cushioned in preferences. Like a gourmand, you're very selective about what you eat and how you eat it. "Organic," you say, as you cut into a little treat with its sugar-free sauce and decorative leaves and flowers and carefully put it into your mouth. Even the seriousness with which the Dharma is approached and contemplated has a sense of stylishness. But where is the wholehearted embrace of the true meaning and essence of Dharma? The stylish approach comes about because we are very clever—clever enough to understand that we would otherwise have to actually practice the teachings.

This is why we have to talk about courage. It takes courage to fully embody the teachings. Without courage, you will hide behind a facade of style. You will walk and talk like a Dharma practitioner, sit like a Dharma practitioner, and become a stylishly serious Dharma practitioner. But while you waste your time styling yourself, inner transformation will be neglected. Then, there you are—endowed with a precious human existence, the ability to understand and practice the Dharma, the ability to generate such pure intentions—and still stricken with habitual neurotic patterns. The ability to wake up and go beyond self-absorption and self-cherishing takes courage.

The mark of degenerate times is what is going on today: What we like to do takes precedence over what we need to do. With this come laziness, doubt, and particularly a lack of awareness.

CONTEMPLATION

Think about your own life and whether or not there is awareness of the preciousness of this human existence. And ask yourself if there is an awareness of impermanence, awareness of your actions, and awareness of the suffering of samsara? Think too about how much distortion is brought into the Dharma when teachings that you have heard and understood are not actually put into practice.

IN DEGENERATE TIMES

Whenever one awakens to innate goodness, it is the dawning of a good eon, a good time.

Someone asked me recently what is meant by "degenerate times." There are so many examples, just in general behavior and discourse, in print and social media, with its emoji, GIFs, and so on—so many of which represent the meanness, greed, ignorance, anger, and sadness of degenerate times. As reflections of the world we live in, they evoke a lot of unkindness and confusion. Of course, it is easy to point out the problems, and it may make you wonder if degenerate times are a done deal. Is this just a fate that we can't do anything about? Do we just go along for the ride, knowing it will be downhill all the way, knowing there's no way out but trying our best anyway?

With a shift of perspective, you might see it another way. Since the only thing you have any control over is your own mind, it is your choice how degenerate you choose to make this mind. As for fate, since fate is something rather personal, you could say that we all make ourselves into our "fated selves"—which are actually not at all fated because at each and every moment we make choices. With the courage to shift your perspective, you could choose to see things a different way.

If someone has an Hermès handbag, for example, you could take joy in seeing a beautiful piece of art or you could scoff at the excessive cost for a piece of leather. You could rejoice for the person who owns and probably loves the bag or you could give in to jealousy or a holier-than-thou attitude that sees it as a waste of money. The moment and the object are the same. You are the one who decides how to ride that moment. As long as you can steer your own mind, there is no need to feel totally under the sway of any form of control.

Degenerate times are not so much about a time, a place, or things. Essentially, whenever one awakens to innate goodness, it is the dawning of a good eon, a good time. Whenever one becomes distanced from that innate purity and relies on extrinsic circumstances for contentment and happiness, it is the dawning of degenerate times. The "times" are about what each one of us makes of today—which is actually not that bad. You and I are alive in today's times, and it is we who will make this a good or a degenerate time. Fate is when you allow conditions to rule you. As His Holiness Trichen Rinpoche once said to my sister Jetsunla and me,

> You can choose to walk on a path made by others. This will be easy, but the path will be the one to decide where you want to go. Or, you can make a new path. This will be difficult, but you will be the one to decide where you wish to go. When you make your own path with wisdom, conditions will never rule you.

I always recall this profound teaching whenever seemingly difficult choices present themselves—especially having found the well-trod path to be more tempting than one realizes.

If you feel strongly the strains of difficult times and the abundant marks of degeneration, you must take it upon yourself to break free from these conditions and to spearhead a new path. What will your contribution be? Your contribution will be to usher in goodness—and if not to destroy degenerate times, at least to delay them. Each one of us has this potential. For one who recognizes this and goes beyond the hurdles of times and conditions, there is time before degeneration actually happens. For those who neglect to see this—degenerate times began a long time ago.

In the Face of What Is Deluded and Not True

As the Buddha himself says in the *Dhammapada*, when you listen to the Dharma, every word must be heard without compromise. There is no compromising with a stylized mind or a mind lacking the courage to let go of convenience. If the Buddha's perspective makes sense to you, you give up speculating about every little thing. Take for example a simple thing like kindness: we may think, "Do I want to be kind or not?" "Why be kind?" or "I'll be kind when it's not so inconvenient."

In the face of what is deluded and not true, truth must be uncompromising. Like a dying person who treasures the last drops of the nectar of immortality, savor every word of Dharma and embody it fully. To engage fully on the path of Dharma, you have to hear, contemplate, and meditate on the Dharma correctly. Meditating is dependent on contemplating, and contemplating depends on hearing the Dharma accurately.

Unfortunately, we all suffer from the habit of closing our ears the moment things become a little inconvenient—and we imagine we can do this forever. When the tendency to hear only what suits your ego persists, inner transformation is very difficult. Inevitably, you become frustrated. The tendency then is to blame your frustration on something or someone else.

Someone who practices the Dharma as Dharma should be practiced would not become frustrated. This is the remarkable thing about great teachers: they never become frustrated—due mainly to never placing blame on anything outside themselves. Imagine these enlightened great teachers surrounded by minds like ours. Do they become frustrated with so many minds lacking in awareness? Did the Buddha become frustrated with people like us? Rather than dwelling on frustration, the mind turns inward. This is what it means to train the mind. Then there is a sense of release and creative possibilities can arise. This is why great teachers never cease to manifest nor cease to find unique ways to inspire us.

This is why all great teachers and bodhisattvas are, for want of a better word, very cool. In the worst of times, they are absolutely cool because the mind has been trained. When surrounded by noise, chaos, and seemingly frustrating situations, they are able to turn inward and to work with it all from the perspective of impermanence, interdependence, and the lack of solidity.

Finding perfection within samsara is almost impossible. So instead of projecting frustration onto all the challenges you face, work with your perspective. Try to see challenges as they truly are. You may not be able to change that, but you can change this. This is what it means to be a practitioner.

CONTEMPLATION

When we think about Shakyamuni Buddha talking to ten thousand people like us, we might think, "What a marvelous environment that must have been!" But to the Buddha, it must have been like talking to ten thousand pillars.

Now imagine you are talking to ten thousand people who are like pillars, knowing full well their potential and how near, yet how far, they are from realizing it; knowing, too, they are not really hearing you and, worse, will not be doing what you tell them to do. If you were in the Buddha's shoes, you would probably be taking antidepressants; at the very least, you would be shaking your head in frustration. Then remind yourself to work with everything from the perspective of impermanence, interdependence, and lack of solidity.

WITH ITS SHARE OF FIREWORKS, BIG AND SMALL

Like all religions, Buddhism has its share of challenges and troubles. I think of them as firecrackers: there are big ones and small ones, but they both explode. Religions with big numbers like Christianity and Hinduism have big explosions. Buddhism, with its smaller numbers, manages to have small explosions, some years more than others.

Some years, beautiful communities face situations that are not easy. In recent times, issues big and small have crept into many communities. Many things have happened that should not happen, and this breaks our hearts. It is heartbreaking because these communities are what we rely on as objects of refuge. With a raw mind and heart, one genuinely takes refuge in what one sees as an object of basic sanity. There is tremendous trust when one turns toward a view that is seen as pure, as that which will allow us to come out from anger, desire, confusion, pride, and jealousy. When, for whatever reason, that trust is shattered, it is as if a part of our heart is ripped out.

In an imperfect world, adverse situations happen. This is samsara. No matter how pure and untainted the teachings may be, they must be sustained in an imperfect world. This in no way justifies any cause of pain or abuse. It in no way justifies any breach of trust, particularly the trust placed in devotion. In no way does it justify not safeguarding ethics and truly refraining from bringing confusion or pain to others. But it does mean that we need to be pragmatic.

The primary responsibility of a community is to extend a loving atmosphere to everyone, particularly to anyone who has experienced pain and heartbreak—without pretending that everything is okay. Whatever one's personal beliefs may be, it is the responsibility of a community to respect the beliefs of others. We will never all always agree. Even when things seem to be fine, there are disagreements. Disagreements are not an issue; they are part of our human nature in samsara. Diverse experiences, opinions, and interpretations of situations are the prerogative of every individual. And if nothing else, there needs to be an honest approach to listening and respecting the diversity of experience. This takes courage.

Maintaining courage in samsara is incredibly difficult, but this is the path of a practitioner. Who better to relate courageously to the adversities that arise? Let's say you were to achieve enlightenment. What then? Having developed unwavering awareness, an enlightened being would never cause harm. If this is your aim, your practice should be in line with the fruition you wish to achieve. These times call for each one of us to unearth the bravery and sanity inherent within us and within our communities.

In the face of "fireworks," it is always remarkable when teachers and community members are able to maintain steadfastness and clarity of vision. Without belittling, whitewashing, or disrespecting those who have suffered through experiences that should never have happened, we must also be very clear about all that we have received. What would it mean to have inherited such a wealth of wisdom, if we didn't treasure it in the most crucial moments? If all that we have studied and aspired to accomplish cannot manifest when most needed, the fault is ours. If our stance is defensive or we sink into denial, it is our own inability to be brave in adverse circumstances. At the end of the day, when faced with painful situations, we can do one of two things: we can allow that situation to collapse every effort that has been otherwise wonderful or we can hold on to what is sane and good and still untainted.

For the sake of future generations, we can continue making rights out of wrongs as best as we can—and even then adversities will arise. Like us, future generations will have good moments and challenging moments. To forget the greater vision that binds Dharma practitioners together would be a terrible loss—not only of many, many years of hard work but also of the blessings, presence, and teachings of all the great teachers of all the various traditions. This isn't a way of whitewashing or denying painful issues. This is a reminder to those of you who have heard so many words of wisdom to not forget to treasure and understand their perspective.

In an imperfect world, it is always advisable to calm down and give things a bit of space. Everything and everyone deserves that space. In community, you could enjoy sitting down calmly and being a little more tolerant and patient with one another. In a practice community where the teacher may be absent, instead of wondering what the teacher would say, or do, or write, you could just provide some space.

This is not about "pacifying" a situation. It is about releasing the tension from a situation. There's a difference! Releasing tension from a situation is the result of training the mind. When you use your own self-cherishing as your reference for understanding others, you understand its pull. You see your own intolerance of any threat to your happiness, you see the importance of your own hopes and fears, and you understand the power of these habitual tendencies. This sympathetic understanding of others takes work. But this kind of work brings a release of tension and allows for something more inspiring to develop.

We can see the challenges facing our civilization; we can see the greed, hatred, violence, and discontent spreading throughout the world. In the face of such challenges, it is wonderful to be able to remain devoted, diligent, and focused. Otherwise, how would things progress into the future for oneself and for the world at large? At times such as these, when the four essential aspects of human civilization itself—economics, politics, spirituality, and the environment—are in trouble, how else would inspiration arise? As a human being who truly aspires to happiness for yourself and others, now is the time to watch your mind. By generating the good thoughts, you will generate good speech and communication, which translate into good actions and good physical causes of happiness.

The Power of Prayers and Aspirations

For the sake of the future generations who will inherit this planet, if you are so inclined, you might consider offering prayers and good aspirations. Instead of just practicing from an intellectual perspective, in the face of the challenges to human society and civilization, it is important to consider the power of supporting the Dharma in the form of prayers and aspirations.

In the Buddhist tradition, prayers and aspirations embody the qualities of the Buddha and the Dharma, and they call to mind those who have realized these qualities. Thus prayers and aspirations can serve as a support or reference for the path of practice. They can remind us of the view; they can remind us of the qualities to cultivate and abandon and the aspirations to generate. And they can remind us how to truly practice meditation—without manipulating meditation with self-cherishing agendas, even seemingly good ones.

When it comes to the reading or reciting of prayers, it is about what you connect with and how you connect with it—if at all. Prayers should never be read with a sense of obligation and not as if prayer alone will benefit you on some level. Rather, prayers should be read with a sense of voicing the view of Dharma. In this way, they serve to support your mind on the path of practice. The important thing is to allow your practice to really blossom in your mind and to make it beautiful. This is how one should relate to prayers.

CONTEMPLATION

If you are wondering how prayers or aspirations might translate into action, you could look at it from the perspective of the eightfold path. Right view is the understanding of how and why we're caught in the cycle of suffering called samsara. Right action is the path, or action, to take.

From this perspective, you would need to do two things to bring your aspirations to fruition. First, work to lessen self-grasping. Second, take the support of the teachings, practices, prayers, and aspirations that have arisen from the wisdom of those who have actually realized them. Have confidence that you too could be the holder of such positive tools for fulfilling this life. How else could you have confidence in the possibility of attaining realization and liberation from suffering for yourself and other sentient beings? Be encouraged to know that you hold in your hands the power to realize this aspiration.

When a Teacher Dies

Just as challenging situations are never wanted, death is never wanted. But the greatest kindness a teacher can actually show to a student is to die. It is important to understand this. Our teachers may be incredibly brilliant. Think back to the two greatest teachers: Shakyamuni Buddha and Padmasambhava, the Indian yogi renowned for bringing Buddhism to Tibet. But we cannot stay attached to the idea of being students, basking in the sun-like radiance of great masters. A teacher's death will test how far you yourself have come as a lineage holder.

When after fifty-three years in Tibet, Padmasambhava was about to take his leave, his students all clung to him. His main student, the yogini Yeshe Tsogyal; his twenty-five heart disciples; and the king of Tibet—all greatly realized in their own right—beseeched him not to go. It is actually great fun to read how each of them begs Padmasambhava, also known as Guru Rinpoche, to teach, in short, all that he had been teaching for more than fifty years! This is how the famous prayer called "Seven Chapters of Supplication to Padmasambhava" originated. Today, Guru Rinpoche's response to their supplications is called the "profound teachings," his pith instructions to his students. But what is also palpable is the students' unwillingness to let go.

It is incredibly difficult to let go of the sense of comfort, blessings, and protection of having lived with a great teacher for many years. When a teacher actually dies or takes leave of the students, suddenly the ground on which you stood is no longer there. Then everything you have been hearing and thinking intellectually is tested through personal experience. Through this personal taste of the teachings, your maturity is tested.

We all go through this kind of experience, like little birds pushed out of the nest. There is the reluctance of the baby bird that doesn't want to be pushed and the kindness of the mother who pushes you. There is the utter panic of not knowing how to fly and the flapping of not fully formed wings. But birds learn to fly. They may plop down, but they come out of it. This is our situation when we are pushed from our comfortable nests, full of enlightened ideas and incense and bright colors. No matter how beautiful the nest might be, it is still a nest. Call it a concept, call it a nest, it's the same.

In today's samsara, as people become more oblivious to their inherent basic goodness, the strength of merit decreases. The ubiquity of confusion, ignorance, and neuroses increases, and waking up may take the kindness of a mother bird kicking you out of your nest. So, when you are thrown out of that nest, whether or not your wings are fully formed—flap them! And make sure that wherever you crash is soft ground because that is probably the only choice you will have.

APPEARANCES ARISING AS ENEMIES OR FRIENDS

There's a saying in Tibetan, *nangwa dra ru lang*, which means "appearances arising as enemies." *Nangwa* means "appearances," and *dra ru lang* means "arising as enemies." You wake up in the morning and everything seems to be antagonistic and against you. Occasionally appearances might arise as *drog*, or "good friends," but when I was growing up, it was much more the case that appearances arose as enemies. I think back to how grumpy I was for the first half of my life, with such a bad attitude. On a really bad-mood day, my teacher, my father, would sit on his bed laughing and waving his hand at me in the way that he had, saying "Nangwa dra ru lang." Appearances had arisen as enemies.

When you don't take teachings to heart and remind yourself to actually embody them, the untrained mind will fixate on antagonistic appearances. This builds frustration. If you dwell on your frustration, it will percolate and become very discouraging to your path of practice. So, work to see things as they really are. Then, instead of saying things like, "Why are others not more kind?" you might ask yourself, "How kind am I?" Ultimately, it comes down to your perspective.

I sometimes ask a few people to be my spies, especially when a group is sitting around the dinner table. This is not to hear what you're saying; I'm not interested in that. I am interested in the tone of what is being said. Sometimes the feedback is pessimistic. The tone may be inclined to be more negative than positive. This is a self-discouraging attitude—in which case, you need to work to cultivate a practitioner's view. A true practitioner holds the view of Dharma in every moment. If you are not careful about how you hold the view of Dharma, your life and the Dharma will be like two parallel train tracks: your life on one track and Dharma on the other, running side-by-side. If they never meet, you will never be able to bring this precious human birth to full fruition.

Since we are all growing older, it is absolutely important not to waste the time we have now. Being mindful of impermanence, if you are not doing Dharma, what are you doing? What have you done in just the last year that you can really boast about? You might find that the last three hundred and sixty-five days have just been bad photocopies of the days before. Doing the same thing over and over is like making the same boiled potatoes every day. Some days you add salt; some days you add pepper or a little chili. Otherwise, it's the same. Meanwhile time passes, and the continuity of distractions and lack of mindfulness leads to an enormous waste of this precious opportunity.

Not wasting time doesn't mean that you should start meditating, reciting mantras, or doing sadhanas twenty-four hours a day. You can continue to boil those potatoes; that doesn't need to change. What does need to change is the quality of your heart and mind. It is your heart and mind that must relax with frustrating appearances and learn to make friends with them. It is you who must embody bodhichitta and manifest kindness. All the qualities spoken of in the context of Dharma are qualities you must cultivate within yourself. There is not one that need not be fully embodied. Not wasting time comes down to understanding that Dharma is not a commodity. Dharma is something you have to be.

THE REMARKABLE TRADITION
OF SELF-EMPOWERMENT

This is the most remarkable characteristic of the Buddhist tradition. As a human being, you are capable of empowering yourself.

Mindrolling Monastery, which is where I come from, is also home to the Great Peace Stupa. Inaugurated in 2002, it is the world's largest stupa. Surrounded by 108 smaller stupas, it is a remarkable example of Buddhist architecture, with wonderful artwork inside. On the other hand, the stupa is very big and flashy, and many of my Buddhist friends were against it from the start. "How much will it cost to build that?" they'd ask, and "Why don't you build a hospital or school instead?" Another way to look at it is this: The stupa stops your mind. Faced with 108 gleaming white architectural objects that you don't even have words for, you might stop what you're doing with a sense of "What is that?" This is a powerful moment of awareness.

At some point, the human mind just needs to stop and rest in a moment of awareness. This may be the beginning of your journey on the path of practice. Something may simply stop your mind, wake you up, and bring you to a powerful moment of awareness. My wonderful Italian friend Stefania became a Buddhist because a book fell on her head. She was browsing in a bookstore one day, when *The Tibetan Book of Living and Dying* hit her on the head. That was bonus number one. She put the book back and went on looking around. When she came back to the same spot, the very same book fell on her head again. Being Italian, she took this as some kind of omen or sign—but of what? So she bought the book and took it home. This was Stefi's introduction to the Dharma.

In order to discover something that is subtler and more difficult to articulate, sometimes the human mind just needs to stop. In Tibetan Buddhism, certain objects are said to "liberate upon seeing." Certain sounds, such as mantras, are said to liberate upon being heard. This is true and very helpful. For that purpose, Buddhist shrines and paintings and statues are good; those bracelets with mantras on them are also wonderful. At a certain level, they do have a purpose. They plant a seed. It has only taken Tibetan Buddhism roughly twelve hundred years to make the brilliant teachings of Dharma into something religious, to hang them on the walls and put them on thrones and shelves—but this is good. It has its purpose. Maybe a book will fall onto your head and introduce you to what we are all trying to understand.

Each of us must come to the point of simply resting in that moment of awareness, without scratching our heads and asking, "What is she talking about?" What brings you to this moment could be a teacher, a practice, a statue, or a painting. It could be some interesting gift from India, Tibet, or Kathmandu—or a book that falls on your head. Eventually, you will come to the point of being able to empower yourself with this awareness.

This is the most remarkable characteristic of the Buddhist tradition. As a human being, you are capable of empowering yourself. You yourself can transcend the doubting mind that does not see its own enormous intelligence and potential to be the cause of happiness and cessation of suffering. The whole Buddhist tradition, no matter which school of thought, is born from this understanding. All streams gather into this single ocean. All the many Buddhist methods and teachings are about empowering yourself to find inner strength and contentment and thus design the field of your own experience.

Until then, you will search for happiness outside of yourself, but you won't find it. The wealthiest and most powerful people, surrounded by every conceivable material comfort, have not necessarily found happiness. Yet there are people without much food to eat or nice houses to live in who are simply happy and content. For example, I live in India, which is a remarkable place—most remarkable for the small moments of glorious happiness and bursts of the loudest of songs and deepest laughter, which is rare in more proper societies of London or Boston. Of course, we all have ways of finding bits of happiness. But Dharma is about finding the cause of happiness and the cessation of suffering within oneself. This will determine how you see and experience things.

I remember well from my Catholic convent school days, a Father Cornelius came to lead a class. I later found out he was quite famous, but for us fifth and sixth graders, he simply brought a glass of water to class. We were asked to look at the glass and the amount of water inside. He then made a list of our names and how each of us saw it: half empty or half full. This is the perspective we're talking about here. What is your perspective on life? When you wake up in the morning, do you see a beautiful day and wonderful people with the good fortune to be human beings endowed with such positive potential? Are you bursting with enthusiasm to make this the best of days for yourself and everyone around you? This is one perspective.

Or, do you wake up to CNN and Fox News? Nothing much good to say there: there are things that could go wrong, things that aren't right, people who don't understand each other, craziness and chaos everywhere—and the temperature's not going to be your liking. It is up to you which perspective you choose. If you are able to see every glass as half full, this is the basis of goodness. This is where courage, patience, hope, and optimism come from.

Ultimately, the Dharma belongs to you. Good or bad, like it or not, it is your Dharma. If you give yourself the luxury of abandoning Dharma the moment things become inconvenient or difficult, you are missing this quality of ownership. A good example of having no sense of ownership: the rats that are the first to abandon ship when the ship's about to sink. If the Dharma is your truth, ask yourself if you really feel you own the Dharma. And if so, what does that actually mean?

Here's an example of a parallel kind of ownership you already have: You do own samsara. No matter how inconvenient samsara gets, rarely do you say, "I want out." It's like being stuck in a bad relationship. On one hand, you think you are stuck in that world because that is your world. On the other hand, you could exchange that world for Dharma. Instead of thinking, "This is my world of samsara," you could think, "This is my world of Dharma. This is the truth that I treasure." And because you treasure what you own, you feel responsible for it.

Without a sense of owning the profound view of Dharma, what we value most will be self-absorption, samsaric worldliness, and convenience. Then, any need for commitment, diligence, or embodiment of the teachings will seem like an imposition of rules and regulations. And everything will feel forced: we force ourselves to come to teachings, we force ourselves to practice. And then we begin to barter.

In olden times, there was no currency. You would barter: when you needed oil, you would exchange something for oil. Likewise, some students try to barter with the Dharma. They will say to a teacher, "If you don't come, I won't practice." They'll barter to do three out of the ten things the teacher said to do—and then ask, "Do I have to do it twice a month or is once a month enough?" This is the way some students are. Bartering with the Dharma originates from a lack of responsibility for your own mind, your own liberation, and the liberation of all sentient beings.

When you treasure and hold the truth of your mind as most important, a natural sense of responsibility arises. The most natural thing to do then is to fully engage and embody the qualities of Dharma. No one has to encourage you to be disciplined or to bind you with commitments. You yourself are naturally responsible for the upkeep and embodiment of the truth that you value.

The Flourishing of Dharma in the West

The flourishing of Dharma in the Western regions of the world is a popular topic in Buddhist circles. But as for the future of Dharma in the West, who else would embody this but those who live there? It is not acceptable to think that change can only be brought about by a teacher, that you cannot bring about change on your own. Teachers come and do their jobs, good or bad, but the Dharma is not held by teachers. Dharma is held in a vessel: the vessel is the country, the culture, and the people who embody the view of Dharma.

It seems that the karma of sentient beings and the karma of the world are going through a transition. It seems that the container for holding the Dharma in the future is fast forming in the West. This flourishing of Dharma may make some people very happy— but it may not always bring an awareness of the responsibility that comes with it. From the teachers' perspective, teachers must realize that conveying genuine Dharma is not just about speaking in various languages or translating texts. It is about the continuity of the stream of the essence of Dharma. The essence of Dharma is what must flow into the West, in the most pure and authentic way. This requires much more dedication and much more understanding of what it means for Dharma to come to the West. Teachers must realize this responsibility.

Students must realize that this flourishing of Dharma is not something to simply be happy about. Expressions of happiness and joy, alone, are not sufficient at this point. Now you must understand that what you are building in the West is something you must have the courage to hold and be responsible for.

Having received the teachings in the most authentic way, now we must all continue—in a very changed world—to hold the truth of their depth and purity in an unbroken way. This calls for both teachers and students, of this generation and the next, to understand the profoundness of what the westernization of Buddhism actually means, for oneself and the world we live in.

Buddhism did not land like a meteorite in the West. If that were the case, you could point to it and say, "Look, Buddhism just landed!" Nor is the coming of Dharma a commodity, nor is it something indicated by certain structures or styles. The presence of Dharma is indicated by the people who embody the view of Dharma. What this means is that you live like a Dharma practitioner. You are someone who speaks more thoughtfully and frees the mind of negativity. And this is the kind of environment and culture you create. If you were sitting in one of those dance studios with mirrored walls, this is the reflection you would see. The mirror would reflect the quality of Dharma in the West today. This mirror might actually work better than a shrine.

The Western practitioners I know have tremendous devotion and even better diligence. The amount of giving up, letting go, and sacrifices they've made to treasure and value the Dharma does not go unnoticed. Collectively and individually, they have invested an incredible amount into the vision of Dharma. They travel long distances to sit in front of a teacher and listen calmly to what's being said. This is what has brought Dharma this far. But now they must go further because Dharma is not a belief system. Dharma has to be owned and accomplished.

Although the power of the teachings is such that with one text, one phrase, one mantra, you could get enlightened, until the teachings fully penetrate and permeate your life, the skin of habitual patterns will never be shed. Beyond an emotional or intellectual connection to Dharma, there must be the transformation of a samsaric being into the qualities of a bodhisattva. This is what the Buddha saw to be the fundamental responsibility of a human being. And because our human lives are interconnected with the lives of others, this was his view of social responsibility.

Whatever practices you do, let every movement you make in life be a complete opening up of yourself, free from grasping and clinging. Then your every move will be a meditation. And when your every thought and word is connected with awareness, then every hour you spend sitting in meditation or doing other practices will have meaning. Then you will be able to walk out into your life and abide in that awareness. This speaks to the training of your mind.

CONTEMPLATION

Dedicated study and staying quietly with your practices both have their virtue, and both lead to a flourishing of Dharma. But ask yourself if your connection to Dharma is truly as it should be. Is it an emotional connection? Are you inspired by the truth of the teachings—without actually going through the necessary changes to train the mind from anger to patience, jealousy to joy, arrogance to simplicity and without waking up to the responsibility of a human being living on this planet? To go into the teachings in depth, you must be willing to practice the teachings correctly and to embody them fully. Then the fruition of Dharma will never be impeded.

EIGHT

Placing Your Two Feet on the Ground

You can study Buddhism and then get the point; or you can get the point and then study Buddhism.

WHATEVER YOUR BACKGROUND, Buddhist or not, I urge you to pledge to truly train your mind. With or without any additional teachings, just work with your own self. This human life is a very precious life. The wonderful qualities of the human mind can be a source of immense happiness for yourself and everyone you relate to. It is not that you have to continually think about liberating all sentient beings, although that would be good. You could just be a sane human being. That would be a great blessing for your own world and the world we all live in.

The view taught by Shakyamuni Buddha is based upon your own taste of the truth of impermanence, interconnectedness, and the emptiness nature of all things—beyond which there is peace. From this perspective, practice has nothing to do with outer appearances, worldly or Dharmic. Relying on outer appearances would put you in danger of not understanding the Buddha's intent or deriving any real benefit from practice.

Practice has to do with your direct understanding of the truth of Dharma. When Dharma is the truth you have confidence in, then outer appearances—whether they arise as enemies or friends—do not have the power to obstruct the truth that you own and value. In the words of the great eighteenth-century yogini Jetsun Mingyur Paldron,

> When you make the outer world too important, there is no way the mind will remain within the understanding of the illusory nature of everything as it arises. But when the mind rests in genuine understanding of its true nature, it doesn't matter which way the world turns, or how the world does or does not work. It is entirely up to you and how you view it.

At the time of her death, Mingyur Paldron was called the Great Bliss Warrior of Supreme Means. During her life, she was often haunted by the experiences of her youth, particularly the destruction of Mindrolling Monastery, founded by her father, Terdag Lingpa. When the monastery was razed during the Dzungar Mongol invasion of Tibet, the vast numbers of Dharma teachings so carefully gathered and preserved there faced extinction. This made Mingyur Paldron work tirelessly to preserve the precious authentic Dharma—undaunted by the challenges of great danger, exile from her homeland, and ill health.

Whatever your background or path, Mingyur Paldron's life and wisdom and message of basic sanity speak to the difficult times the world faces today. Like her, you could commit to preserving the authentic essence of Dharma in your mind and heart. Waking up in the morning, you could think to yourself,

> Just like the Buddha, I am placing my two feet on the ground.
> May the earth bear witness to the sincerity of my commitment.
> May my every step actualize the benefit of sentient beings—
> Knowing that this cannot happen until my mind is tamed.

Ultimately, nothing is as real as we think. Ultimately, we are not as separate as we think. And ultimately, there is no real basis for the clinging, grasping, and ego-cherishing that is ignorance, the cause of suffering. Realizing this brings a sense of humility and also a sense of relief. If you work sincerely and decisively to tame your mind in this way, you can be quite sure the practices will refine the view within you. Then you will not just be thinking about being good, kind, and enlightened. Whichever way the world turns, you will be able take the teachings into your everyday life. In this way, you could bring about true change and benefit for yourself and others.

What would be the greatest real benefit for the world and all the beings within it? In the end, it would come down to an understanding of the impermanence, interconnectedness, and emptiness nature of things. To put this understanding into practice: "Do no harm, do everything virtuous, and train your mind. This is the view of Buddhadharma." This speaks directly to our responsibility as human beings.

But keep this in mind: When you talk about meditation and developing mindfulness, awareness, and so on, what you have undertaken is the very essential approach of knowing your own basic nature—and through that, being able to illumine your world with the qualities of kindness and compassion. Whether you do this in a simple way or a progressive way, the choice is entirely yours. This is what brings about the diverse approaches to the study of Buddhism. Ultimately, they all gather into a single essence: your natural ability. To recognize this is called Dharma; to not recognize this is simply called ignorance. So, according to your own inclination, aptitude, and what makes sense to you, you can study Buddhism and then get the point or you can get the point and then study Buddhism.

Whatever your path, this is the way we human beings can bring our best and most meaningful aspirations down to earth.

Editor's Acknowledgments

Many wonderful people helped to bring these oral teachings into the form of the book you now hold in your hands. First and foremost, heartfelt thanks to Mindrolling Jetsun Khandro Rinpoche for unfailing generosity and wisdom and to Mindrolling Jetsun Dechen Paldron for astute advice and encouragement along the way. To the many transcribers of these teachings, whose names were never known to me, and to Zuzana Dankova, who helpfully gathered select teachings given by Rinpoche in Europe, many heartfelt thanks. For formative editorial expertise and insights, I am very grateful to former Shambhala Publications editor Sarah Stanton. For significant editorial assistance from afar, sincere thanks to Steve Iverson. For generous contributions of time and valuable insights, many thanks are due to Judy Wolfer and to readers of the manuscript: Jann Jackson, Landon Shaw, Cheree Hammond, Ellen Lebowitz, and Meg Federico. For significant contributions and thoughtful conversations, thank you to Alex Ryan, Julie Heegard, Michael Vader, and Barbara Ryan. And finally, greatest appreciation and gratitude to Nikko Odiseos and the outstanding Shambhala Publications production and editorial staff, most especially Shambhala editor Anna Wolcott Johnson, all of whom patiently and knowledgably brought this book into a form worthy of the content. May the fruit of these endeavors be of great benefit.

Helen Berliner
Mindrolling Lotus Garden
Stanley, Virginia
2024

Tibetan and Sanskrit Terms and Names

PHONETIC SPELLING	TRANSLITERATION	ENGLISH
alaya (Skt.)	ālaya	base, ground
Ananda (Skt.)	Ānanda	name of a disciple of the Buddha
anatman (Skt.)	anātman	no self
anitya (Skt.)	anitya	impermanence
Arada Kalama (Skt.)	Arada Kalama	name of a teacher of the Buddha
atman (Skt.)	ātman	self
bodhi (Skt.)	bodhi	enlightenment
bodhichitta (Skt.)	bodhicitta	mind of enlightenment, aspiration to enlightenment
bodhisattva (Skt.)	bodhisattva	a realized one whose motivation is the benefit of sentient beings

PHONETIC SPELLING	TRANSLITERATION	ENGLISH
Brahma (Skt.)	Brahmā	name of a god in Indian religion
Brahman (Skt.)	Brahman	the highest rank in the Indian caste system
Buddha (Skt.)	Buddha	"the awakened one"
Buddhadharma (Skt.)	Buddhadharma	the teachings of the Buddha
Charvaka (Skt.)	Cārvāka	name of an Indian philosophical tradition
chipa, chirolpa (Tib.)	phyi pa, phyi rol pa	"outsider," non-Buddhist
dag yig (Tib.)	dag yig	grammar, orthography
depa (Tib.)	dad pa	devotion
Dharma (Skt.)	Dharma	teachings of the Buddha
digpa (Tib.)	sdig pa	unvirtuous action
drog (Tib.)	sgrogs	good friend
drowa (Tib.)	'gro ba	movement, going
drowa semchen (Tib.)	'gro ba sems can	sentient being
duhkha (Skt.)	duḥkha	suffering
Dzogchen (Tib.)	Rdzogs chen	Great Perfection
gewa (Tib.)	dge ba	virtue
geweshenyen (Tib.)	dge ba'i bshes gnyen	spiritual teacher, "virtuous friend"
guru (Skt.)	guru	teacher, lama

Hinayana (Skt.)	Hīnayāna	Foundational Vehicle
Jamyang Khyentse Wangpo (Tib.)	'Jam dbyangs mkhyen brtse'i dbang po	name of a nineteenth-century Tibetan master
karma (Skt.)	karma	action, act
Kashyapa (a.k.a. Mahakashyapa) (Skt.)	Kāśyapa (Mahākāśyapa)	name of a disciple of the Buddha
khatag (Tib.)	kha btags	offering scarf
klesha (Skt.)	kleśa	afflicted emotions
Lankavatara Sutra (Skt.)	*Laṅkāvatāra Sūtra*	*Sūtra of the Descent to Laṅkā*
Madhyamaka (Skt.)	Madhyamaka	"Middle Way" philosophical tradition
Mahamudra (Skt.)	Mahāmudrā	"Great Seal" meditation tradition
Mahayana (Skt.)	Mahāyāna	Great Vehicle
marigpa (Tib.)	ma rig pa	ignorance
Mindrolling (Tib.)	Smin sgrol gling	familial lineage name of Jetsun Khandro Rinpoche and monastic site
Mingyur Paldron (Tib.)	Mi 'gyur dpal sgron	name of an eighteenth-century meditation master and daughter of Terdag Lingpa
mogu (Tib.)	mos gus	devotion and respect
muni (Skt.)	muni	sage
Nagarjuna (Skt.)	Nāgārjuna	name of a first-century Indian philosopher

PHONETIC SPELLING	TRANSLITERATION	ENGLISH
nangpa, nangpa sanggyepa (Tib.)	nang pa, nang pa sangs rgyas pa	"insider," Buddhist
Nangwa dra ru lang (Tib.)	Snang ba dgra ru langs	Appearances arising as enemies.
nidana (Skt.)	nidāna	steps, stages
nyamlen (Tib.)	nyams len	practice
Nyingma (Tib.)	Rnying ma	Ancient Tradition
nyon yi (Tib.)	snyon yid	afflictive consciousness
Padmasambhava (Skt.)	Padmasambhava	name of an Indian master
rangrig (Tib.)	rang rig	self-awareness
samsara (Skt.)	saṃsāra	cyclic existence
sangha (Skt.)	saṃgha	Buddhist community
Shakyamuni (Skt.)	Śākyamuni	"Lord of Sages," epithet of the Buddha
shamatha (Skt.), zhine (Tib.)	śamatha, zhi gnas	peaceful abiding meditation
Shariputra (Skt.)	Śāriputra	name of a disciple of the Buddha
shepa (Tib.)	shes pa	consciousness
Shuddhodana (Skt.)	Śuddhodana	name of the father of the Buddha
Siddhartha (Skt.)	Siddhārtha	"He Who Achieves His Goal," personal name of the Buddha
Songtsen Gampo (Tib.)	Srong brtsan sgam po	name of a seventh-century Tibetan king

sutra (Skt.)	sūtra	teaching or sermon of the Buddha
Tathagatha (Skt.)	Tathāgata	Thus Gone One, epithet of the Buddha
Terdag Lingpa (Tib.)	Gter bdag gling pa	name of an eighteenth-century Tibetan master
tulku (Tib.)	sprul sku	"emanation body," incarnation of a past master
Udraka Ramaputra (Skt.)	Udraka Rāmaputra	name of a teacher of the Buddha
Vajrayana (Skt.)	Vajrayāna	Diamond Vehicle, Adamantine Vehicle
vipashyana (Skt.), lhagtong (Tib.)	vipaśyanā, lhag mthong	"clear seeing," insight meditation
yana (Skt.)	yāna	vehicle
Yeshe Tsogyal (Tib.)	Ye shes mtsho rgyal	name of a female Tibetan master
yiche (Tib.)	yid ches	confidence
yogini (Skt.)	yoginī	female practitioner
zagche (Tib.)	zag bcas	contamination
zhenrig (Tib.)	gzhan rig	awareness of other
zogom (Tib.)	bzod sgom	meditation on, or familiarization with, patience, or tolerance
zopa (Tib.)	bzod pa	patience, tolerance

Index

asceticism, 13
aspirations, 33, 56, 126–28, 141.
    See also bodhichitta
attachment, 39, 43, 81, 87. *See
    also* self-attachment
awakening, 20, 47
    Ananda's, 113
    Buddha's, xiv–xv, 13, 21, 25
    meaning of term, 13
    of others, 65
    See also enlightenment
awareness, 67, 125
    absolute, 107
    afflicted, 106
    ground consciousness and, 75
    impediments to, 55
    in meditation, 72
    and mental consciousness,
        relationship of, 71
    resting in, 74–75, 76, 131, 132
    in samsara, maintaining, 116
    sympathetic understanding
        and, 61
    tolerance and, 54, 55
    two aspects of, 72–73
    of virtue and nonvirtue, 53
    virtue as result, 59

basic goodness, 57, 129
    basic badness and, 114
    confidence in, 42
    potential for, 17, 31
    recognizing/discovering, 3, 35,
        100
    as ultimate nature, xiv
    of world, 115
basic sanity, 43, 124, 140
beginners, advice for, xvii
    on feel-good Buddhism, 6
    on ground consciousness,
        experiencing, 75

on meditation, 57, 72
on tolerance, 61
birth
    link of (*nidana*), 28
    suffering of, 10, 24
blessings, 90, 97, 125, 128, 139
bodhi mind, 61, 65. *See also*
    wisdom mind
bodhichitta, 106, 131
    aspiration, 64–65
    conceptual understanding of, 62
    tolerance and, 54
bodhisattva path, 42, 55, 65
bodhisattvas, 136
    as cool, 55, 123
    fixed identity, lack of, 56
    motivation of, 16
body
    innate purity in, 41
    in meditation, 56, 78
    movement of, 47, 48
    unvirtuous acts of, 30, 32, 39,
        40, 44
boomerang effect, 53
Brahma, 19
breath, 31, 56, 73
Buddha. *See* Shakyamuni Buddha
buddha nature, xiv, 31, 84, 87,
    98, 100
Buddhadharma, xvii
    pillars of, 101
    purity of, 92
    purpose of, 82
    Shariputra's verse on, 37–38,
        40, 42, 43, 53, 67, 78
    study and practice, balancing, 94
    See also Dharma; Dharma
    practice
buddhafields, 107–8
buddhahood, 13, 14. *See also*
    enlightenment

buddhas, 9, 13, 16, 17, 89, 98
Buddhism
    candyfloss, 6, 111
    cultural influences on, 10
    diversity of approaches, 68, 141
    essence of, 3, 4, 10, 110, 135
    fireworks (challenges) in,
      124–26
    first schism in, 112
    institutional, 92–94
    interest in, xiii, 5
    as label, xvi
    loyalists and true practitioners,
      distinctions in, 20
    and other religions, distinctions
      in, 101
    as perspective, 7, 9
    preconceptions about, 4
    purpose of path, 31–32
    and science, distinctions
      between, 14
    traditional teaching method, 15
    treadmill, 6–7, 111
    true practitioners of, 20, 44, 130
    See also Dharma; Tibetan
      Buddhism; westernization of
      Buddhism
Buddhist communities (sanghas)
    Buddha's, 111–12, 113
    loyalty in, 91
    responsibilities of, 124–26

causes and conditions, 21–22, 23,
    25, 84, 102
Charvaka philosophy, 19
Christianity, 8, 124
clairvoyance, 13, 116
class division, 12
commitment, 31, 134, 140
common consensus, 108, 109, 110
compassion, 3, 25, 43, 64, 141

beliefs about, 4
perspectives on, 7
relaxation and, 108
selfless, 15–16
of spiritual teachers, 85–86, 87
spontaneous arising of, 43
from sympathetic
    understanding, 62
complications, fondness for,
    114–15
compounded things, 102–4, 105
concepts, 57, 96, 129
    limitations of, xiv, 62
    not grasping at, 58
    solidifying, 109
    susceptibility to, 4, 81
    teachers' ability to cut, 84–85, 95
conditioning, 13, 17, 42, 110,
    121–22
confidence, 6, 140
    to allow goodness, 116
    devotion and, 88
    in direct experience, 97
    in impermanence, 103
    naturally arising, 118
    in realization, attaining, 128
    in teacher-student relationship,
      91
    virtue and, 42, 96
    weakening, 114
confusion, 18, 52, 93, 124, 129
    conditioning of, 13, 17, 31, 82
    of degenerate times, 120
    meditation and, 57
    neutral attitude and, 69
    in teacher-student relationships,
      85, 97
consciousness
    Hindu view of, 12
    link of (*nidana*), 27, 28
    sleep and, 75

Dharma practice, 34
   courage in, 86, 119–20
   direct understanding in, 140
   holding view in, 130
   as inner guru, 86
   meaning of, 117–18
   meditation's role in, 83
   methods of, 35, 84
   responsibility in, 135–36
diligence, 57, 84, 96, 98, 99, 134,
   136
direct experience, xv, 6, 7, 62, 97,
   101, 118
discontent, 10, 19, 24, 81, 82, 126
Discourse Requested by Maitreya,
   The, 89
discrimination, 78
   afflictive consciousness and, 75
   ground consciousness and, 76
   of mental consciousness,
      69–70, 71, 72, 74
   right mindfulness and, 30
   sympathetic attitude and, 61
dissatisfaction, xvi, 12–13, 44,
   45, 60
doubt, 16, 85–86, 98, 106, 114,
   120, 132
Dungse Rinpoche, 109
Dzogchen, 75, 110

ego, 23, 114
   afflictive consciousness and, 69
   biases of, 115
   emotions and, 106
   investigating, 78
   mistaken tolerance for, 59
   persistence of, 122
   in teacher-student relationships,
      95, 97, 99
   in understanding others, 65
ego-cherishing, 65, 141

ego-grasping, 76. See also
   self-grasping
eight levels of consciousness,
   68–69, 77–78. See also
   afflictive consciousness;
   ground consciousness (alaya);
   mental consciousness; sense
   consciousnesses
eightfold path, 26, 34, 127
   basis of, 32
   contemplating, 35
   right action, 29, 127
   right concentration, 30–31
   right effort, 29–30
   right livelihood, 29
   right mindfulness, 30
   right speech, 29, 35
   right thought, 29
   right view, 26–28, 32, 35, 127
emotions, 83
   afflicted/contaminated, 59, 91,
      101, 105–7, 108
   in Buddhism, connecting with,
      6, 136, 137
   as impediment to awareness,
      55
   mental consciousness and, 71
   self-absorption and, 42
   solidifying, 104–5
   in teacher-student relationships,
      87–88, 95, 96
   unvirtuous acts and, 39
empathy, 46, 60, 62, 64
emptiness nature, 22, 101, 108
   benefit of understanding, 141
   intellectual comprehension,
      109–10
   in Madhyamaka analysis, 102
   as natural law, 24, 25, 34
   one's own taste of, 139
   of self, 76

mindfulness meditation, 6, 28
Mindrolling Jetsun Khandro
   Rinpoche. *See* Khandro
   Rinpoche
Mindrolling Monastery, 131, 140
Mindrolling Trichen Rinpoche,
   His Holiness
   on appearances arising as
      enemies, 129–30
   on Buddhism, xiv
   on miracles, 115–16
   on path, 121
   "This too will pass" mantra
      of, 103
miracles and magic, 13, 115–16
monkey mind, 70–71, 73–74
movement, 51, 55
   impatience and, 59
   interconnection and, 52–53
   meditation as antidote to, 72
   mind and, 67, 70
   sentience and, 47–48
   with and without choice, 49

Nagarjuna, 54, 102, 110
name and form, link of, 27
nature of mind, 4, 31–32, 39, 43,
   90, 110, 140
neurosis/neurotic patterns, 4–5
   Buddha's insight into, xvi–xvii
   increasing, 129
   limitless, 52
   mistaken tolerance for, 60
   teacher's role with, 97
neutral attitude, 69
nihilism, 19
nirvana, xvi, 107, 111
no self, 21. *See also* emptiness
   nature
nonconceptual realization, 14
nontheism, 15, 16

Nyingma lineage, 87
old age, suffering of, 10, 24
opinions and judgements, 74, 115,
   124–25

Padmasambhava (Guru Rinpoche),
   128
patience, 43, 84
   compassion and, 25
   developing, 30, 137
   innate capacity for, 113
   responsibility for, 49
   in right thought, 29
   source of, 133
   of students, 98, 99
   of teachers, 97
   as tolerance, 53–55, 59, 61
*Pattern of the Stem Discourse,
   The*, 90–91
peace, 33, 101, 111, 139
perception, three energies of, 70
permanence, 34, 102, 109
philosophy, xiv, 5
prayers, 126–27
precious human life, 17, 33, 39,
   49, 58, 119–20, 139
pride, 93, 106, 114, 124
primordial pictures, 60
projections, 27, 73, 123
pure self/soul, 12, 18–19

refuge, 38, 45, 124
religions, 8, 14, 44, 45
religious attire, 5–6, 7

samsara (cyclic existence), xvi, 53,
   82, 123
   courage within, 125
   familiarity with, 31
   movement of, 47–48
   ownership of, 134

samsara (cyclic existence)
(*continued*)
   realization in, 116
   right view of, 26–28
   suffering of, 63
self, 11, 43
   afflictive consciousness and, 76
   impermanence of, 53
   karma and, 22
   letting go of, 32–33
   prioritizing convenience of, 45, 46
   reflexive momentum of, 41–42
   threats to, 52
   virtue and, 41
   See also pure self/soul
self-absorption, 42, 54, 56
   afflicted awareness in, 106
   contracting into, 52, 58
   going beyond, 120
   mistaken tolerance for, 59
   valuing, 134
self-attachment, 16, 76
self-awareness, 70–71, 72–73
self-cherishing, 53
   as cause of suffering, 32, 34
   freedom from, 15, 42
   transcending, 43, 120
   transforming, 61–62, 64, 65
   in understanding others, 126
   virtue and, 57
self-discipline, 40, 42
self-grasping, 16, 127
selfie culture, 104–5
selflessness, 15, 32, 39, 54, 58–59
sense consciousnesses, 41, 47, 68, 69, 70, 72, 74, 77–78
sensory experiences, 68–69, 70–71, 72, 74, 75, 82
sentient beings, xiv, 13
   Buddhist understanding of, 47

movement of, 49
responsibility, levels of, 50
sameness of, 62
understanding, 64–65
separateness, myth of, 46
"Seven Chapters of Supplication to Padmasambhava," 128
Shakyamuni Buddha, 128, 139
   awakening of, 13, 21, 25
   dissatisfaction of, xvi, 12–13, 44, 45
   eighty-four thousand teachings of, 43
   intent of, xiii, xiv, xv, xvii, 38, 43, 45, 46–47
   intent of, forgetting, 11
   life story, 9–10, 18
   perspective of, 8, 14
   simplicity of teachings of, xv
   successor of, 111–12
   teaching method of, 15, 16, 89
   throws his cup upstream, 117
shamatha meditation, 56, 73, 78
Shariputra, 111
Shariputra's four-line verse, 37–38, 40, 42, 43, 53, 67, 78
Shuddhodana, King, 9, 10
sickness, suffering of, 10, 24
sitting meditation. *See* meditation
six senses, link of, 27–28
skillful means, 43, 83, 87, 92
social responsibility, xvii, 41, 46–47, 115, 136
solidification, 22–23, 25, 27, 34, 104, 109
Songtsen Gampo, King, 40
speech, 126
   innate purity in, 41
   in meditation, 78
   movement of, 47
   right speech, 29, 34, 35

About the Author

Mindrolling Jetsun Khandro Rinpoche holds the lineages of both the Nyingma and Kagyu schools of Tibetan Buddhism. As the daughter of Kyabje the eleventh Minling Trichen, Jetsun Khandro Rinpoche holds the authentic lineage and transmissions of the Mindrolling lineage. At the age of two, Rinpoche was also recognized by His Holiness the sixteenth Karmapa as the reincarnation of the Great Dakini of Tsurphu, Ugyen Tsomo. Today, Rinpoche heads the administrations of Mindrolling Monastery and Samten Tse Retreat Centre in India.

Mindrolling Jetsun Khandro Rinpoche is one of the most renowned teachers of Tibetan Buddhism. Since the early 1990s, she has been teaching students in the West and is the author of the book *This Precious Life: Tibetan Buddhist Teachings on the Path to Enlightenment*. As the head of Mindrolling International, Rinpoche established Mindrolling Lotus Garden in Virginia, the Western seat of Mindrolling, and many centers and study groups in the West. Thus, Rinpoche's vast Dharma activities continue to benefit countless beings in whatever way is most helpful.